SUBURBITAT

JIM TOLSTRUP

Library of Congress Control Number: 2024907758
Paperback ISBN: 978-1-7372523-1-3
Ebook ISBN: 978-1-7372523-2-0

High Plains Environmental Center

All proceeds from this book support the environmental stewardship
and educational mission of the High Plain Environmental Center.

DEDICATION

---

*To Kathy Williams-Tolstrup, my wife of 40 years,
and to the nature that we love.*

ACKNOWLEDGEMENTS

Edited by Julia Mathien and Marly Cornell
Book Design by Ryan Scheife, Mayfly book design
All photos by High Plain Environmental Center unless otherwise noted

Special thanks to the following people

High Plains Environmental Center Board of Directors
Jen Bousselot, Greg Holman, Greg George (Chairman), Ken Morgan, William Timpson, Lisa Yamane

High Plains Foundation Board of Trustees
Denise Bretting, Joe Knopinski (Chairman), Paul Mueller, Alan Pogue, Rich Shannon

HPEC Staff
Sabrina Kershman, Kristin Oles, Pam Sunderland, Jack Van Vleet, and all past, present, and future HPEC/HPF board members and staff.

Past HPEC directors:
Ripley Heintz, Patricia Waak, and Keith Desrosiers

McWhinney Team
Jeff Briedenbach, David Crowder, Wendi Cudmore, Chad
McWhinney, Troy McWhinney, Jim Niemczyk, Kim Perry, Celeste
Smith

HPEC Friends and Advisors
Eric Blewitt, Anita Comer, Daman Holland, Tom Hoyt, Kelley
Jazdzewski, Panayoti Kelaidis, Alison Peck, Phil Phelan, Lauren
Sadowsky, Roger Sherman, Ross Shrigley, Scott Skogerboe, Ray
Sperger, David A. Tolstrup, Brian Vogt

Landscaping with Colorado Native Plants Conference Partners
Jennifer Bousselot, Deryn Davidson, Rhonda Koski, Lisa Olsen, Lisa
Roundtree, Irene Shonle, Susan J. Tweit, Denise Wilson, Amy Yarger

Waptúǧa Thiyóšpaye kiŋ na Lakȟóta Oyáte kiŋ wópila tȟáŋka
wičháwak'u.

HIGH PLAINS ENVIRONMENTAL CENTER MISSION

The High Plains Environmental Center works to educate communities to become replicable "living laboratories" which demonstrate restorative examples of land stewardship, native plants, and wildlife habitat.

CORE VALUES

Collaboration. Economic and environmental interests can be mutually beneficial. We work with people from all walks of life and divergent points of view and are dedicated to facilitating meaningful dialog about stewarding our natural world.

Conservation. We focus on science-based practices that conserve natural resources, emphasizing water conservation and native plants that support wildlife.

Education. Through educational programs, we enhance awareness and knowledge of how to live sustainably in our world.

Communication. We propagate an environment of trust both within our organization and beyond and strive to create a culture of respectful and effective communication as a model for others.

CONTENTS

SECTION I: THE STORY OF THE LAND

SECTION II: RESTORING NATURE

SECTION III: A CULTURE OF ENVIRONMENTAL STEWARDSHIP

FOREWORD

Panayoti Kelaidis in the "tulip gentian patch" at HPEC

As a keen wildflower lover, the tulip gentian (*Eustoma grandiflorum*) was something of a quest for me: aside from cactus blossoms and the prickly poppy, this has to be the largest flowered, showiest wildflower native to the Great Plains. Poppies and cacti have survived human-caused decimation from the spread of cities and farming on the plains, and even somewhat adapted to some of our disturbance, but the vast fields of tulip gentians that could once be found along all the various creeks and rivers in Eastern Colorado fared far worse. I watched in dismay as one habitat after another that I'd discovered where this species still persisted were destroyed: a shopping center was built in the mid-1980s on the last colony that still grew in the Denver metropolitan area (just north of I-70 and Kipling). A colony of deep violet tulip gentians just west of I-25 at the Longmont Exit along the Saint Vrain is now a vast gravel mine. One by one, each location disappeared, a grim testament to how nature gives way to the human-dominated Anthropocene age.

In late July of 2016, I had my first visit to the High Plains Environmental Center (HPEC). It was on a bus field trip I'd organized with Jim Tolstrup for members of Denver Botanic Gardens. I shall never forget when Jim pulled out his phone and showed me a vast field of bright-purple tulip gentians he told me were blooming at HPEC! I was stunned: "Why on earth didn't you tell me you had such a treasure on that property?"

Jim went on to explain that they'd suddenly appeared that year after he and his crew painstakingly cleared the property of weeds and reestablished the native community of grasses, sedges, and riparian shrubs along the lakes. The process had apparently exposed the long-dormant seed of the tulip gentians buried in the seedbank, and suddenly they just appeared in vast numbers! I will never forget that afternoon as our merry busload of nature lovers cooed and gloried among the silken purple chalices of *Eustoma* flowers that positively glowed in afternoon light, dotting a long stretch along the margins of the HPEC lakes.

This is for me a sort of fable—almost a true-life fairy tale. Something rare and endangered has been restored! It is emblematic of the many miracles occasioned by the creation of the High Plains Environmental Center. It shattered my cynical illusion that humanity and nature represented a dichotomy, for here a housing development had in fact restored a delicate habitat where a plant I'd feared would one day disappear instead has returned.

In 1920, for the first time, more Americans lived in cities than in the country. The process has accelerated since then, although suburbs as we know them now were negligible a hundred years ago. It was only after the Second World War that vast areas around every urban center in the United States and Canada exploded with planned suburban communities. Since then suburbs have expanded exponentially. They've become the quintessential human habitat for North Americans. Almost twice as many of us live in suburbs than live in urban centers—and there are four suburbanites for every rural town or farm dweller in America. North America today could well be renamed "suburbia."

For the first century of our history, the United States was a nation of farmers and small-town folk. Cities were small and held a fraction of the population. Practically everyone was familiar with crops and orchards: if you didn't raise them yourself, your aunts, uncles, or grandparents were likely still on a farm that you would visit. Most farms had wild woodlots, and most towns and even cities were not far—sometimes walking distance—from wild places like ponds.

Suburbs are now universal. They're also controversial. They combine the best and worst of city living and rural areas. The homes in most subdivisions are, by definition, relatively new with the latest conveniences—isn't that the American dream after all? But just as developments are master-planned using relatively few blueprints, suburban home designs often lead to monotonous repetition. The "dark side" of suburbia is no secret to most of us. The deadening architectural uniformity that Malvina Reynolds parodied so well in her classic song "Little Boxes": the ranch-style home on a quarter acre is deemed the dream and goal of all red-blooded Americans, but at some point or another, everyone comes to worry about the vast tracts of land given over to "little boxes, little boxes, little boxes made of ticky-tacky."

The redundant houses are surrounded by similarly uniform plots of land that are (if anything) even less inspired and less diverse than the homes themselves. The palette of plants of *Hortus suburbica* is often based on what's sold by the local big-box stores. These are in turn produced by nurseries in faraway places—and the same plants are sold across the country—so that a suburban landscape in Boise, Idaho, can look much the same as one in Louisville, Kentucky.

Douglas Tallamy in *Bringing Nature Home* points out that suburbia is essentially a toxic desert when it comes to plants and the birds and other living creatures that actually sustain our ecosystems. Rather than connecting the city to nature, the suburbs have become a sterile buffer that further separates the city from what fragments of nature remain between one city and the next.

Commuter rail and automobiles are, of course, the reason suburbs came about in the first place. There is a great cost to the transportation systems that created and sustain the myth of the suburb: vast sums are spent to build highway and rail networks and continue to be spent to pay for their maintenance. Fossil fuels are still much of the basis of vehicle travel and the cost for obtaining and maintaining vehicles themselves can be added to the tally. And let's not even tally the fossil fuel costs of heating sprawling suburbs. And let's not even think about the environmental costs in water, pesticides and fuel to maintain the sterile "green" spaces of a suburb.

We'd like to think of suburbs as a human amenity, but suburbia, much like technology, is what is driving America. The history of the United States as a country has really been the history of conquest and alteration: as Robert Frost puts it, "The land was ours before we were the land's."

At this point, we as humans have altered or affected practically every centimeter of the continental United States—often transforming what we have conquered unrecognizably. Once we have conquered, what's next? Suburbia has already swallowed up much of America's best bottomlands that produce our food. But even suburbanites need to eat! Will we pave every last truck farm for more houses?

Philosophers and therapists have identified "nature deprivation syndrome" in children who grow up in sterile, plantless cities and a suburbia that is comprised of asphalt, concrete, bluegrass, and a few alien shrubs. Not just environmentalists, but everyone is starting to dread and resent the cancerous spread of suburbs. Platting for them is increasingly in the crosshairs of planners who now argue for infill, and for ethnic, social, and economic diversity in human habitats.

The vision of this book is a glowing example of how we can pivot and transform the vision of suburban habitats from sterile, ex-urban enclaves of mediocrity into something once deemed unimaginable: actual bridges that span humanity and the natural world. The suburbitat described in this book is a prime example, really a model of just that: due to the vision of an inspired developer, teaming with a network of city planners, businessmen, and a wise local government entity that created HPEC, that has provided a nexus. HPEC is the nerve center for a mosaic of multiuse: suburban homes, businesses, office parks nestled among beautifully preserved and restored natural environments.

The process outlined in this book has culminated in something remarkable: a suburban habitat that integrates and honors the surrounding ecological systems. HPEC is the guiding force that is evolving into something altogether new to city planning: a land management entity that is effectively a botanic garden, a native plant nursery, a center for education of children and adults about our native environment, and a social center for the community. HPEC is the answer to Robert Frost—this is how we can give ourselves back to the land.

This book is a blueprint, the sort of visionary promise that presents a *hypothesis: suburban habitat that is ecologically sound and satisfying for a particular community can be created through inspired city planning and execution.* The *antithesis* is demonstrated by the challenges the team has faced in restoring derelict spaces, building the infrastructure of HPEC, and the obstacles overcome to bring the community to understand this novel vision. The *synthesis* is manifest if and when you visit HPEC and see houses and commercial buildings that are settled into a matrix of the very landscape that was here before human settlement: long ribbons of native shortgrass prairie between the homes, expansive parklike spaces that recreate all the ecosystems of the Eastern plains from restored wetlands full of rare wildflowers to upland hillocks covered with shrubs and tufted grasses. And studding the necklace of green spaces and parks there is the visitor center where the community can converge for talks and classes to learn about our natural and human history, gardens that honor the first peoples who settled the region, community and display gardens to hone the neighbor's skills for their own plots of land, and a native plant nursery that supplies garden enthusiasts throughout the region.

HPEC is nothing short of a sterling model of inspired development. *Suburbitat* gives me enormous hope that one day, suburban developments are no longer buffers, but bridges between the world of nature and humanity.

—Panayoti Kelaidis, Senior Curator and Director of Outreach, Denver Botanical Gardens, and coauthor of *Steppes: Plants and Ecology of the World's Semi-arid Regions*

PREFACE

The Education of a Gardener

As far back as I can recall, I have been fascinated by plants and took great delight in learning the names of local plants when I was young. Many of the plants that I learned about were weeds; although many of them, such as Coltsfoot (*Tussilago farfara*), had once been important medicinal plants in European herbal lore. My father, a man of intense and ever-changing fascinations, shared in this passion for wild plants for a time. One summer, after reading Euell Gibbons' *Stalking the Wild Asparagus,* we ate a lot of wild-crafted experiments, including cattail pollen pancakes.

I am very much a child of *Suburbitat* (the natural habitat within the built environment). For a portion of my childhood, I lived in Indiana. At the age of five, I could walk out of my suburban home and explore creeks and farm fields amid the encroaching subdivisions. I recall stick insects and moths that seem huge in memory, finding box turtles and hognose snakes, and learning to eat papaws that fell from the trees. I have an early memory of standing by woods at the edge of our driveway, gazing in wonder at the fireflies all around.

Later, in Massachusetts, I wandered the woods at the edge of a golf course and caught turtles, frogs, and fish at Towner's Pond, 25 miles away from Thoreau's Walden. I collected animal skulls, feathers, stones, and plants. I craved nature as a child, but I was nowhere near truly wild places. We lived at the edge of Boston. The night sky glowed

Towner's Pond

from thousands of streetlights, not the stars of the Milky Way. Amidst the buildings and telephone wires, I trained myself to look only for trees, plants, granite outcroppings, and any natural beauty. This quality became useful later as a landscape designer and photographer.

My woods were farmlands abandoned after World War II. In my lifetime I have seen an oak forest grow from trees that were not much taller than I was. E.O. Wilson, the Harvard biologist, called the New England forest the "ecological wonder of the twenty-first century." Massachusetts was 90 percent agricultural in 1900. By the end of the century, it was 70 percent forest. Setting aside the food security issues implied by this change in land usage, the "wonder" is that this forest regenerated itself to a large extent. The recovery of the shortgrass prairie where I now live is a much more challenging proposition due to the arid environment. It will not likely be achieved any time soon without human intervention.

I was perhaps at a generational cutoff point for outdoor play. Although my fishing and wandering were not entirely unique among my peers, it made me different enough from other kids to earn me the nickname "Mother Nature's Son," like the Beatles song.

Howard Gardner, a developmental psychologist and researcher, proposed that humans possess nine different types of intelligence. Naturalistic intelligence is a reference to how sensitive an individual is to the world of nature. This is an inclination that adults involved in ecology and nature education can observe in children. When I was around nine or ten years old, I clearly remember seeing an elderly woman working on a watercolor painting of a chickadee at Drumlin Farm Preserve in Lincoln, Massachusetts. As I watched her paint, she looked up at me for a moment, and our eyes met. Many years later, I recognize in that moment the look that older people have when we see the spark of curiosity about nature reflected in a child's eyes.

My career in horticulture began with raking leaves and doing small projects for our neighbors. I had a vegetable garden in our backyard, and I always knew that I preferred being outdoors whenever possible. After working for various landscapers, I eventually started my own small business growing flowers and then designing perennial gardens in Kennebunk, Maine. It was not until I was already in the garden design business that I began to formally study horticulture at the Arnold Arboretum of Harvard University, where I received a Certification in Gardening Arts. My instructors at the Arnold were among the leading plantsmen in the country, including Michael Dirr and Darrell Probst.

My clients in Maine were mostly wealthy summer residents. The most notable among them were George H.W. and Barbara Bush, former US president and first lady. I designed and maintained gardens at Walker's Point, President Bush's "Summer White House" in Kennebunkport Maine, for eight years. I have a box full of handwritten notes about zinnias, lilies, and other favorite flowers, as well as numerous cards and thank-you notes from Barbara Bush, including one from Camp David written on Christmas Day.

In May, I would prepare the flower garden, which was not the least bit style-conscious or trendy. Like the Bushes themselves, the garden was straightforward, old-fashioned, and practical. It was a place where Mrs. Bush loved to cut flowers for her house on bright summer days.

Once a year, my presence was requested for an in-person walk

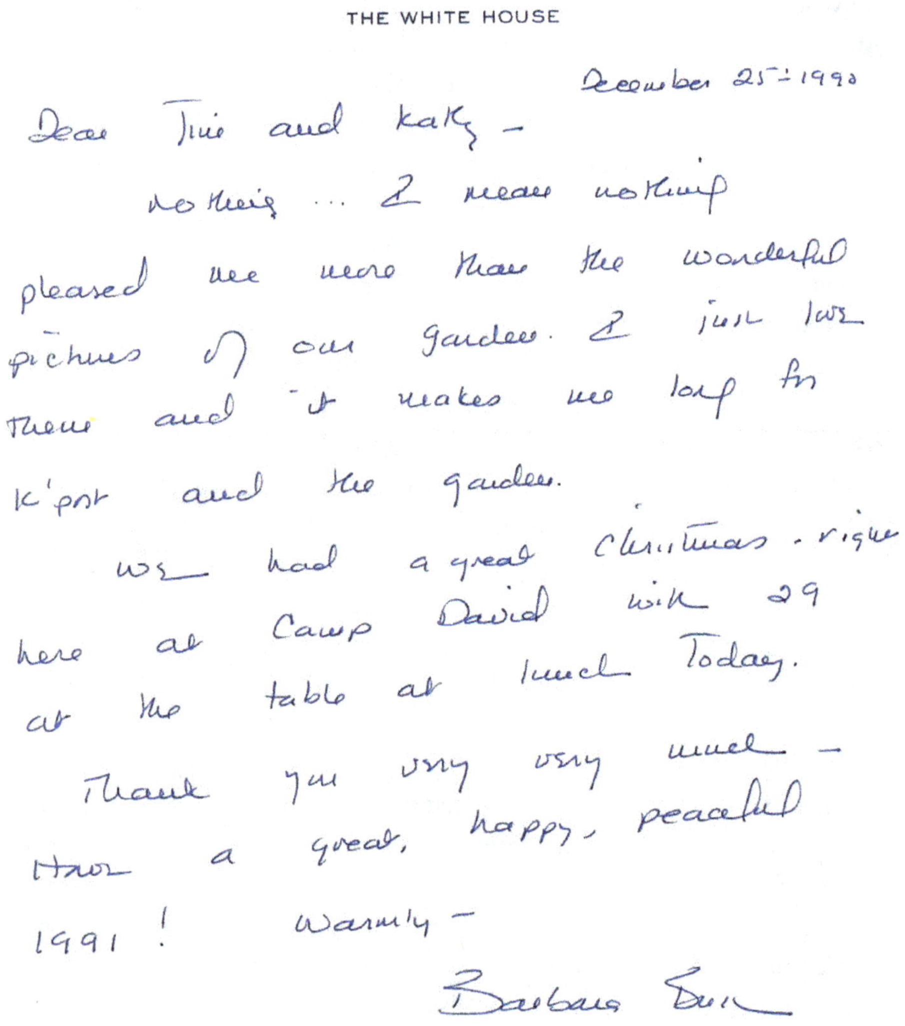

THE WHITE HOUSE

December 25 - 1990

Dear Trici and Katy —

nothing ... I mean nothing
pleased me more than the wonderful
pictures of our garden. I just love
them and it makes me long for
K'port and the garden.

We had a great Christmas - right
here at Camp David with 29
at the table at lunch Today.

Thank you very very much —
Have a great, happy, peaceful
1991 !   Warmly —

Barbara Bush

Camp David note Christmas Day, 1990

Barbara Bush's garden, 1990 (Photo Credit: Suzanne Stohlman)

around the garden where Mrs. Bush and I chatted about flowers. Sometimes our exchanges were more personal. Once, in her garden, Mrs. Bush glanced over her shoulder at the mobs of people on Ocean Avenue a half-mile away and muttered, perhaps to herself, "I hate my new life." The fishbowl of public life was a challenge for the Bushes. Kennebunkport was where they went to escape and, if not blend in, at least rub elbows with the locals at the Clam Shack. Mrs. Bush would occasionally evade the Secret Service and load her grandkids up in their station wagon to go shopping at Renys, a very down-to-earth department store.

Coastal Maine receives an average of 46 inches of rain per year, and in that moist and humid environment, with ethereal northern light, it's easy to replicate a classic English flower garden with soaring delphiniums and foxglove. Austin, Texas, however is a very different matter.

My wife and I moved to Austin in 1992, where I managed a five-acre

Garden designed by Jim Tolstrup, York, Maine (Photo Credit: Suzanne Stohlman)

private garden for a wealthy family. Picture a suburban-scaled Downton Abbey blocks away from the state capitol "deep in the heart of Texas." As the garden manager, I worked with consultants, Nan Sinton, the education coordinator for *Horticulture* magazine, whom I had met through the Arnold Arboretum; and Penelope Hobhouse, a well-known English garden writer and designer.

In Texas, I not only learned a new plant palette but also a new climate where hardiness meant surviving summer's brutal heat and drought, as well as occasional winter plunges into the teens. After six

Private garden, Austin, Texas

Residential landscape, Fort Collins

years in the Texas heat, we longed for a Northern climate but had become accustomed to the panoramic landscapes of the West.

While living in Texas, I had been to a retreat at the Rocky Mountain Dharma Center, later known as Shambhala Mountain Center, in Red Feather Lakes, Colorado. On my first visit to Northern Colorado, I was struck by the snowcapped peaks in July, and the way the airport shuttle to the retreat center climbed one range of hills after another, each new vista revealing more spectacular wildflowers. Over the next five years, I harbored a secret wish to live in those hills until we moved to Fort Collins in 1998.

I volunteered at the Shambhala Mountain Center for the next three years while working at a Fort Collins nursery designing landscapes. In 2001, the Shambhala Mountain Center hired me as their land steward, and we moved to Red Feather Lakes to live at the Center.

In my opinion, everyone should experience what it's like to truly live in a "community" with others. If that could be in a place where you walk under glittering stars at night, or among wildflowers, deer, and mountain bluebirds by day, it would help to cut through the claustrophobia of working, eating, and showering with the same people day after day. At Shambhala Mountain Center, I managed a property of nearly 700 acres of montane forest and meadows. From our small cottage, which had no running water, we saw coyotes, bobcats, bears, and moose.

With the help of a team of volunteers, we built gardens around the newly constructed campus, tended a large vegetable garden, and created a six-mile trail that encircled the valley. I led land tours and offered talks on natural history and environmental ethics. We met amazing teachers from various world wisdom traditions, including Thich Nhat Han, a Nobel Peace Prize recipient and Buddhist monk, and Pema Chodron, Buddhist nun and author of meditation/self-help books. I had the opportunity to introduce Chief Arvol Looking Horse, a Lakota spiritual leader, to H.H. Dalai Lama in 2006.

At Shambhala Mountain Center, my lifelong love of wild plants became fully integrated into my outlook as a horticulturist and landscape designer. Because of the natural setting and the arid, high-altitude environment, we decided early on to focus on Western native plants.

Shambhala Mountain Center vegetable garden and greenhouse
(Photo Credit: Madeleina Bolduc)

Chief Arvol Looking Horse and Jim Tolstrup (Photo Credit: Frank King - Lisa Balk King)

In a larger sense, we intended to help facilitate a conversation that could lead to developing a unique style of horticulture for the Rocky Mountain West. Toward this end, we hosted an annual garden seminar co-facilitated by Panayoti Kelaidis of the Denver Botanic Gardens. I arrived at Shambhala Mountain as a landscape designer, but I left with a distinctly "restoration ecology" perspective.

When I came to High Plains Environmental Center (HPEC) in April of 2007, I became the fourth executive director of an organization only in its sixth year. The term "suburbitat" was coined by the organization's first executive director, Ripley Heintz. Suburbitat is a portmanteau of the words "suburban" and "habitat." The meaning of the term is that the human environment is our habitat and that we can invite other species to share in that space with us.

It was the notion of habitat restoration in the communities that we design and build that initially attracted me to HPEC. I was inspired by the possibility of creating natural areas and demonstration gardens that could help blur the line between nature and the built environment. However, when I first visited in 2007, the land that comprised the center was in extremely poor condition. It would not be an overstatement to say that much of it was an ocean of weeds with a few pockets of established native vegetation. When I came home from my first visit to the place, my wife asked me what I thought of it.

My response was, "Well, there's nothing to love."

When I think of it now, the gardens filled with wildflowers and shrubs, the thronging pollinators, birds, and abundant wildlife we see there daily, I realize that, after dedicating fourteen years to HPEC, this place has become my joy. I see now how perfectly this reflects the many places in the world with degraded environments that could benefit from love and attention.

The work of restoring nature to the communities that we design and build is ultimately the work of a peacemaker. I bring with me a lifetime of experience in horticulture, but more importantly I bring a deeply ingrained commitment to the preservation of wild species, as well as a respect for the universal human desire to have a fulfilling, dignified, and prosperous life. This type of peacemaking requires patience and a willingness to listen. A thread that runs throughout this book is the willingness to engage with others, to examine our motivations and preconceptions, and to build consensus around conservation, utilizing scientific data to improve the lives of as many beings as possible.

The story of HPEC is, at least in part, a story about reconciliation with the land and its original inhabitants; it is a coming together of past, present, and future united in the intention to preserve this world and its habitants, beings of all sizes and shapes, for future generations. This mission has a particular meaning for me. Another thread from my personal experience that has been woven into the fabric of HPEC is a lifelong affinity with Native American culture. When I was around twelve years old, reading John Neihardt's poetic narrative, *Black Elk Speaks* had a transformative effect on me.

I remember reading about Black Elk, who had a great vision about the powers of the world when he was a boy, while sitting outdoors in my backyard. I looked up and saw thunderclouds crashing together. "The Thunder Beings are real," I said to myself.

From that point on, I wanted to go to South Dakota to meet a medicine man and go on a vision quest. Perhaps I understood intuitively that the vaguely "Protestant for weddings and funerals" background that I had grown up with lacked rites and rituals that could lead a boy across the threshold from childhood to adulthood. I graduated from high school in 1977 and, within a few weeks, I was on a Greyhound bus to Rapid City, South Dakota.

That summer, I did meet a medicine man, Norbert Running of Parmelee, South Dakota. Over the years that followed, I went through the initiations a Lakota youth might undergo; standing on a lonely hilltop for four days without food and water, piercing my flesh in the sun dance, and receiving a name as one of the *Ikčé Wičása* (*eek-chay wee-cha-sha*), the common people.

In 2003, Chief Sam Moves Camp adopted me as a brother through ceremony. The Huŋká ceremony is one of the Seven Sacred Rites of the Lakota. It's the adoption ceremony or "the making of relatives," but it is also sometimes called "killing the enemy" because when they become part of your family; "the enemy" is no more. Sam is a descendant of *Wóptuȟ'a* (*wope-too-kah*), which means "chips." Wóptuȟ'a was an Oglala medicine man of the nineteenth century. He was also the cousin

Chief Sam Moves Camp and Jim Tolstrup at High Plains Environmental Center
(Photo Credit: Gregg Campbell)

of Crazy Horse, whom he helped to obtain a power that made him invincible in battle. Sam is a modern-day cultural treasure who possesses rare knowledge of oral history, treaties, healing, and ceremonies. Once Sam said to me, "Someday you may have to speak up for the land and the people."

When I asked him what I would say, he replied, "You came out of that culture, and you faced death through the sun dance, say what you feel."

The antidote to feeling that we are anything great or powerful is to stand out on the prairie in a raging thunderstorm. There in the wind and hail, we will remember that we are nothing more than a tiny ant crawling on this Earth. Nothing that we own will last. As Sam has often said, "If you don't care about your fellow human beings, you don't know anything." My spiritual practice is to try to see the good in everyone, try to find the points of connection between people, and speak up for those who may not have a voice, including all forms of life, whether plants, birds, or insects.

A few times, Sam and his wife Eileen have visited High Plains Environmental Center. I was excited to show them how we brought the prairie back to life amid neighborhoods and shopping malls. Sam and Eileen smiled to see the medicines, the native prairie plants they know so well, reintroduced here in a rapidly developing area. A flock of geese flew overhead, and Sam looked up, murmuring as if to himself or perhaps to someone else, present yet unseen, "This is Jim's world."

The environmental stewardship evident in the 3,000-acre, mixed-use development called Centerra, in Loveland, Colorado, results from a unique collaboration between a 501(c)3 nonprofit High Plains Environmental Center and a developer, McWhinney. This symbiotic relationship between economic and environmental interests provides a hopeful vision for conservation in the twenty-first century, focusing not on conserving wild places that already exist but also on restoring habitat within the communities we design and build.

Our story would perhaps be of interest on a local level alone if it did not contain a replicable model that can be applied virtually anywhere. The elements within this story are universal, including the tensions between economic growth and environmental protection, the drive for a comfortable standard of living, and a deep desire to maintain our connection to nature, which has sustained humanity from our primordial origins. We believe that our model can provide immediate benefit to one of the world's most pressing environmental problems, the issue of growth vs. conservation. It was our inspiration to provide a working example for reconciling wild and constructed environments so that others could replicate it in their communities and regions. This book is the offering of our twenty years of experience in this endeavor.

THE STORY OF THE LAND

Longs Peak and Mount Meeker are named for two white men of the nineteenth century:
Nathan Cook Meeker and Major Stephen Long. The ancient Arapaho name for them is
nesótaieux (the two guides).

CHAPTER 1

PRIMORDIAL ORIGINS

There was a sea, a vast, shallow, salty sea. In that sea, there existed creatures that we could not imagine, even in our wildest dreams. The 34-foot-long elasmosaur paddled around the warm sea, feeding on fish and aquatic invertebrates. The remains of these ancient animals can be found in places like the Badlands of South Dakota. Native people are aware of these remains but seldom touch them. "Do not disturb *Unktéȟi* (*unk-tay-hee*) the water monster," the Lakota elders warn, "or you may bring calamity on your home."

Slowly the land began to rise as the continental plates collided, creating the highest mountains on the continent, like a backbone through the center of North America. The tilting tablelands created "hogbacks," lengthy ridges with steep sides called the Dakota formation all along the front range of the Southern Rockies. The friction of the geological collision created hot springs throughout the region, and to the east, a sea of grass began to emerge. Thus the High Plains were born.

Over time, reptiles transformed into megafauna, giant mammals: bears, bison, mammoths, and sloths. One hundred thousand years ago, the cheetah taught the frightened pronghorn antelope to be the second-fastest land animal on Earth, and they're still running today. In a period ten to twenty thousand years ago, the megafauna began to die out, possibly because of the arrival of hunting bands of human beings. However, some anomalies show human remains from a much earlier period.

Lindenmeier site

The Hopi people who live in Northern Arizona say that they walked through the "back door of the continent" and traveled south through a vast and lonely land. Other native people say that they have always been here. A Lakota origin story says that they emerged from the *Unči Makȟá* (*oon-she mah-kah*), Grandmother Earth, somewhere in the Black Hills, following their elder brother, *Pté* (*ptay*), the bison.

Situated 28 miles north of Fort Collins, Colorado, is the Lindenmeier Site, one of the oldest and most significant archaeological sites in North America. The site, which lies within the city's Soapstone Prairie Natural Area, is important because of the technological innovation that it represents. Folsom points, a particular type of carved stone projectile, were found there in great abundance. Folsom points were an innovation because the fluted center of the points allowed them to be solidly attached to a spear for throwing and making them a more-penetrating weapon.

The site had many advantageous characteristics that supported the people who lived there. A sheltering ridge to the north for protection from winter winds. A creek ran through the area, which would have provided fuel from cottonwood trees, as well as water. Another

Jasper hide scraper found in Larimer County, CO

important reason for this site's popularity was its visibility. The smoke from a campfire could be seen from many miles away. Jason LaBelle, an archeologist at Colorado State University, says that there were very few people at that time, and there are few or no signs of conflict or violence. People sought out other human bands in that lonely land to find mates and trade for goods. The jasper points for which this site is famous were carried from hundreds of miles away.

In their search for food and trade, ancient people crossed the Continental Divide through a particular route that did not involve a steep climb. This east-to-west route, which is just 10 miles north of the Lindenmeier Site, is now Interstate 80, and continues to connect the two sides of the Continental Divide. The Overland Trail of the 1800s traversed much the same route. The area was a crossroads, north and south along Colorado's Front Range and east to west across the Great Divide.

Native American tribes in the region were migratory because the grassland environment required a vast area to support the wild game on which they depended. The Lakota also called *Očhéthi Šakówin* (*oh-chety sha-koh-ween*), or "seven council fires" of the western Siouan speaking peoples, occupied the territory directly to the north, from the headwaters of the Missouri River to the Powder River, a span of over 300 miles. In winter, the Lakota camped along the banks of the North Platte River.

Like the ancient people at the Lindenmeier Site, the Lakota of the nineteenth century found shelter with ridges to the north, water, fuel, and cottonwood twigs to feed their ponies in winter. In spring, these people migrated west to hunt bison in the Powder River Basin, stopping along the way to perform spring ceremonies at various sacred sites. The ceremonies culminated with the sun dance at Devil's Tower, called *Mathó Thípila* (*matoh-tee-pee-lah*), "the bear's lodge," by the Lakota.

Arapaho and Southern Cheyenne tribes moved up and down along the Front Range. The Pawnee, and their traditional rivals, the Lakota, frequently clashed in Eastern Colorado and Western Nebraska. The seven Ute bands ranged throughout present-day Colorado on both sides of the Continental Divide.

A strange new people came out of the East in the early 1800s, and by the end of that century, the tribes no longer wandered freely.

In 1803, President Thomas Jefferson commissioned the Lewis and Clark Expedition to explore a vast area of the American West, land that the young nation was purchasing from France. The expedition traveled up the Missouri River then overland until they reached the Columbia River, and the Pacific Ocean thirteen months later. The expedition crossed the High Plains through the present-day Dakotas and Montana.

Lewis and Clark described the land they traversed as follows: "Low ground has a fertile soil of rich black loam . . . the drier situations are covered with fine grass, tansy, thistles, onions, and flax. The uplands . . . only produce prickly pear, the sedge, and the bearded grass, which is as dry and flammable as tinder."

The expedition of Major Stephen Long, in 1823, crossed a more southerly route, which included Colorado, and produced a map labeling the area as the "Great American Desert." The party's geographer, Edwin James, wrote in an accompanying report: "I do not hesitate in giving the opinion, that it is almost wholly unfit for cultivation, and of course, uninhabitable by a people depending upon agriculture for their subsistence. Although tracts of fertile land considerably extensive are occasionally to be met with, yet the scarcity of wood and water, almost

Devil's Tower, called *Matȟó Thípila* (*matoh-tee-pee-lah*), "the bear's lodge"
by the Lakota

uniformly prevalent, will prove an insuperable obstacle in the way of settling the country."

In 1851, the United States government signed a treaty with the tribes in the region, at Fort Laramie, on the North Platte River. The US sought to secure a safe route for settlers to pass through this "worthless" region on their way to more "habitable" lands. The treaty was the first official agreement between the tribes and the US. It was intended to secure "an effective and lasting peace" and guaranteed rights of ownership to the tribes "as long as the grass shall grow." The treaty included an annuity to be paid to the tribes and extended the right for the U.S. Army to build a series of forts at key points, particularly along rivers, in the region.

The treaty council, held near present-day Morrill, Nebraska, included the Lakota, Cheyenne, Crow, Arapaho, Assiniboine, Arikara, Mandan, Gros Ventre, and Eastern Shoshone.

The Arapaho and Cheyenne were assigned to the lands along Colorado's Front Range, bordered by the North Platte River to the north, and south to the Arkansas River. Historically, the High Plains' indigenous nations' territories, which lay between the Missouri River and the Rocky Mountains, overlapped and shifted. Many of the tribes were traditional rivals who fought frequent skirmishes over control of their respective claims to the territory. Native American conflicts with rival tribes, though deadly at times, served primarily as a reminder of each tribe's strength and autonomy. Unlike wars in European and Asian history, indigenous warfare did not include the overthrow and destruction of other nations. It was often as simple as touching an enemy with a "coup" stick without bloodshed.

The first permanent homesteader in Northern Colorado was Joseph "Antoine" Janis. Janis was born in Missouri in 1824. His father was a French-American fur trader, and his mother was part African American. Janis may have traveled to the area with his father in 1836 to the Cache la Poudre River, named for a lost (or stolen) cache of gunpowder. In 1844, Antoine Janis returned to the area and staked a squatter's claim on the fertile bottom lands along the Poudre, a place he called "the loveliest spot on Earth."

Antoine Janis worked with his brother, Nicholas, as an interpreter at Fort Laramie, where he met and married First Elk Woman of the Oglala. Janis returned to the Poudre River valley with his wife when the area opened for settlement in 1858. His two brothers, Nicholas and Francis, joined him along with a group of settlers and 150 lodges of Arapaho who accompanied them from Fort Laramie. Janis and his companions founded the town Colona, which is now LaPorte, Colorado.

In the same year (1858), Mariano Medina, a scout from Taos, New Mexico, became the first permanent settler in the Thompson River Corridor, in present-day Loveland, Colorado. Like Janis, Medina's wife was a Native American. Medina spoke English, Spanish, and several native dialects. In 1861, Medina began constructing a stone fort, called Namaqua, after members of the Ute tribe raided and stole sixty of his horses.

Coup stick

At Namaqua, built at a convergence of trails, Medina operated a toll bridge, trading post, and stagecoach stop. The site later became a post office. Medina died in 1878. His cabin was restored in the 1920s and is preserved at the Loveland Museum. His grave was moved to Namaqua Park in 1960. A marker was placed in the park near the site of the former stage station.

In 1858, the discovery of gold west of Denver brought a flood of gold miners to the region. Many settlers crossing established trails to the north were either diverted by the lure of gold, or simply grew weary of the arduous trip, and chose to settle on Colorado's Front Range.

John Hahn was born in Germany in 1840. He emigrated to the United States and arrived in Colorado in 1860. He homesteaded on 160 acres of government land three miles east of Loveland. A farmer and businessman, Hahn was the president of the Ryan Gulch Reservoir

Mariano Medina (Courtesy of Loveland Museum/Gallery)

Company and one of the organizers of the Loveland National Bank. Hahn was the great-great-grandfather of Chad and Troy McWhinney, the developers who created Centerra, a 3,000-acre, mixed-use development on the site of their ancestral homestead. Our narrative will continue to track this piece of land, a portion of which would ultimately become High Plains Environmental Center.

CHAPTER 2

THE BREAKING OF THE PRAIRIE

B etween 1861 and 1865, the Civil War diverted the attention and resources of the US government and the territories of western tribes remained more or less intact. By 1880, all indigenous tribes had been "removed" from Colorado except for a narrow strip (15 miles wide and 110 miles long), the Southern Ute Reservation, in the State's southwest corner. On the morning of November 29, 1864, Colonel John Chivington and 675 soldiers attacked a sleeping village of Arapaho led by Chief Niwot and Southern Cheyenne led by Chief Black Kettle, on Sand Creek southeast of Denver. An American flag flew above the village, which was encamped in a place the army had told the chiefs would be safe for them and their people.

Captain Silas Soule, who participated in the peace talks that resulted in the choice of Sand Creek for the Arapaho and Cheyenne Camp, refused to have his soldiers participate in the massacre that followed. Soule recounted the events of the day in a letter, which later became the basis for several congressional investigations into the atrocities at Sand Creek, although no charges were ever filed.

Months after his testimony, Soule was shot and killed on the streets of Denver. His killer was never brought to justice. During a Sand Creek memorial run each year, members of the Southern Cheyenne tribe pause at the intersection of 15th Street and Arapaho Street to remember Captain Soule, who was gunned down on that spot.

Chief Niwot died at Sand Creek. The Southern Cheyenne and

Southern Arapaho were removed to Oklahoma. Chief Black Kettle was killed at the Washita River Massacre in Oklahoma, almost four years to the day after Sand Creek. In 1867, the Northern Arapaho, who had been promised territory in Eastern Colorado, were removed to the Wind River Reservation in Wyoming.

Meanwhile, towns along the Front Range continued to grow. In 1877, the Colorado Central Railroad was constructed east of Namaqua through the new town of Loveland. In 1878, the United States Congress passed a law requiring all Native Americans to be confined to reservations. Antoine Janis was presented with a terrible choice: abandon his family, or leave a prime homestead on the Cache la Poudre River and follow his family to the Pine Ridge agency, where the Lakota struggled to adapt to non-nomadic reservation life. Janis, a man of significant standing among the Lakota, chose the reservation, and he frequently served as an interpreter in important matters.

Janis lived out his life on the reservation and died in St Francis, South Dakota, in 1890, just months before the death of Chief Sitting Bull and the Wounded Knee Massacre. In the present day, numerous Janis descendants live on the Rosebud Reservation. The Janis Cabin was moved to the Fort Collins Library in 1939.

Following the discovery of gold in Colorado in 1858, the number of prospectors in the territory quickly grew to over 30,000. The Utes, who spent summers in the high mountain country, returned to their winter camp grounds to find the land claimed and occupied in their absence.

In 1868, realizing that the Front Range was being inundated with settlers, leaders from all seven Ute bands signed a treaty creating a protected reservation covering twenty million acres in Western Colorado. In exchange for the land ceded to the United States, the Ute people were to receive compensation in the form of an annuity of rations, trade goods, livestock, and other supplies. Chief Ouray (Arrow), of the Tabeguache band, was chosen as principal chief of the Ute Tribe.

In 1874, after silver and gold were discovered in the San Juan Mountains, miners demanded access to the Ute Territory. US representatives forced the Utes to sell about one-fourth of the 1868 reservation for an annual payment of $500,000. The government claimed that the

Antoine Janis (Courtesy of Fort Collins Museum of Discovery)

Janis cabin

miners would flood the territory with or without the treaty. Chief Ouray could not understand why the government could not prevent the settlers from coming and said, "The agreement an Indian makes to a United States treaty is like the agreement a buffalo makes with his hunters when pierced with an arrow. All he can do is lie down and give in."

In 1878, Nathan Meeker was sent from Greeley, Colorado, to establish the White River Agency in Western Colorado. The agency is where governmental affairs relating to the Ute Tribe were conducted. Though not a religious leader, Meeker approached his vision of "civilizing" the Utes with a missionary zeal. Although the Utes could easily survive in their territory through traditional hunting and gathering, Meeker intended to remake them into farmers in the white settlers' model.

Meeker infuriated the Utes by plowing up a meadow used as a track for racing horses. He used his connections at the *Greeley Tribune* to launch a statewide propaganda campaign claiming that the Utes had set fire to white homesteads and declaring, "The Utes Must Go!"

John Long Rout, Colorado's first governor, became enormously wealthy in the San Juan mining operations. Frederick Walker Pitkin, who became the state's second governor in 1878, was also involved as an investor in the mining industry. Neither governor was sympathetic to the plight of the Utes to maintain their land and sovereignty.

A party of Utes, including Chief Ouray, who was now in failing health, went to talk with Governor Pitkin. They told the governor that on their journey to Denver, they had observed with their own eyes a homestead that Meeker claimed had been burned by the Utes. The situation reached crisis level when Meeker wired for military assistance claiming to have been injured in a shoving match following the horse-track incident. The government sent 150–200 soldiers to White River. Realizing they had been betrayed, the Utes attacked and killed Meeker and ten male employees and took women and children as hostages.

By 1881, the Yampa, Uncompahgre, and Grand River Ute bands were forced to leave Colorado. The remaining Ute bands were confined to a small strip of land along the LaPlata River in Southwest Colorado.

In little over two decades, the Indigenous Tribes of the High Plains had been confined to reservations. Their treaty rights and their land continued to dwindle through congressional legislation for another century. For much of the twentieth century, Native Americans were referred to in the past tense as something that "once was," or at best, they were considered an obscure historical footnote of interest but no real relevance. The last Native American boarding school in the US closed in the 1970s. Prior to that, generations of native children were forcibly taken from their families and punished for speaking their ancestral languages or practicing their cultural traditions. In this land, founded on freedom of religion, Native American ceremonies were prohibited by federal law until 1978.

The "Indian Country" of the reservations became a sort of time capsule, preserving both a remnant of the land relatively undisturbed, as well as the cultural model of environmental stewardship based on a sacred relationship that the world has come to know in later decades.

In the present day, Denver has one of the largest urban populations of Native Americans in North America, representing over 200 tribal nations. The 2010 Census Bureau recorded 104,464 people who identify as American Indian alone or in combination with other races living in Colorado.

In the book *1491,* Charles Mann writes about twentieth-century archaeological research, which indicates that Native American populations, before Columbus, were far more extensive than previously thought. He argues that North America had a population somewhere between twenty and eighty million people before the introduction of European diseases for which Native Americans had no immunity. He further posits that the North American continent was a managed ecosystem of forests and grasslands comprising "the largest garden on earth."

There is no question that Native Americans used fire as a tool to thin forests and maintain grasslands, to increase the herds of grazing animals on which they depended for food. Foresters in Colorado say that 80 percent of the state trees are less than 100 years old. The intentional suppression of wildfires over the twentieth century has resulted in a dangerous fuel load that, when ignited, burns not only the understory, removing grass and tree seedlings, but produces a "crowning fire" that burns mature trees down to the soil.

Over 30 million bison once roamed the prairie. Their numbers in the wild were reduced to less than 1000 by 1884.

In the absence of Native American stewardship, the high plains (also called the shortgrass prairie) have been profoundly altered. A story has been repeated so often that its origins are hard to determine if it ever actually occurred, about a Plains Indian watching a white settler plowing the prairie grass under. "Wrong side up," the Indian said stoically. Whatever the original intention of this story may have been, it serves as an astute observation that the prairie sod, once broken, is not easily repaired. Grazing animals—bison, elk, and bighorn sheep—which were an essential part of the grassland ecosystem, were extirpated, and domesticated species introduced in their place. Grizzly bears, wolves, and other predators were eliminated in all but a few areas of the Lower Forty-eight states by the middle of the twentieth century.

Before the damming and diversion of Colorado's rivers, melting snow fed rivers into surging torrents. The "June rise" was so intense that it tore out seedling trees and shrubs and scoured river gravel into bare sandbars. In the absence of this ecological process, the Rowe

Once greatly diminished, populations of sandhill cranes have significantly recovered and can be seen in large numbers during their spring and fall migrations.

Audubon Center in Kearney, Nebraska, has had to create sand bars in the North Platte River to accommodate the half-million sandhill cranes that migrate through the area each year. Eastern bird species, such as the eastern blue jay, have moved into the area, literally hopping from tree to tree up the river corridor.

CHAPTER 3

DIRT FARMS TO DEVELOPMENTS

U nlike other parts of the state, there was little mining in the early days of Northern Colorado; quarry stone, gravel, concrete, and coal mining came later on. Economic development in the area focused primarily on agriculture. Among the challenges of farming on the Front Range were dramatic temperature swings and unpredictable frost dates, and a meager annual precipitation rate of twelve to fourteen inches per year.

Homesteaders diverted water from rivers through shallow channels to irrigate their fields. As agriculture continued to expand in the area, the demand for irrigation began to draw the river flows down to a trickle. Water laws were developed based on a complex schedule of the seniority of rights to irrigate, tied to specific properties. Water law remains one of the founding principles of the state and an issue that controls the fates of municipalities and developments in the present time.

Farming interests led to the formation of water cooperatives along irrigation canals. One such system was owned by a British company called the Loveland and Greeley Irrigation and Land Company. This company purchased a system of canals and reservoirs including Blue Lake, created out of a trade for water rights on property owned by a farmer named Houts. The lake, known today as Houts Reservoir, lies within the lands owned by High Plains Environmental Center.

In 1900, a group of farmers purchased the system of canals and lakes from the British firm for $48,750. According to the Greeley

Equalizer Lake

Loveland Irrigation Company (GLIC), the current owner of this system of irrigation canals and reservoirs, one old-timer reportedly said, "Those British drove a hard bargain, but they've gotta get up with the chickens to get the best of us dirt farmers."

The newly formed GLIC created a second lake called Equalizer, completing the project in 1907. Equalizer was created by building a dam and diverting a canal dug in the late 1800s to flood a low-lying area.

Farmers began eyeing the water that flowed into the Colorado River west of the Great Divide. In 1937, President Franklin Roosevelt authorized federal funds to start a massive engineering project that bored through the mountains and diverted water from the Western Slopes to the Front Range. The project was completed in 1957.

The town of Loveland grew to 2,000 people by the beginning of the twentieth century. Through their hard work and tenacity, the dirt farmers began to prosper, but there was no major industry. The Great Western Sugar Factory construction in 1901 brought an economic boom to

Great Western Sugar Company factory Loveland, Colorado

the area, and farmers began to focus on sugar beets. Soon other sugar mills were constructed in Fort Collins, Windsor, Eaton, Greeley, Long-mont, Brighton, Fort Morgan, Sterling, and other Colorado towns. At one time, twenty-two sugar factories operated in the state.

Farmers who had irrigation available also grew alfalfa, corn, beans, and other crops. Unirrigated lands were used to grow wheat. Colorado State University, a land-grant university founded in 1870, became a major center for education in horticulture. The U.S. Department of Agriculture's Agricultural Research Service (USDA-ARS) opened the Central Great Plains Field Station in 1929 in Cheyenne, Wyoming, where 5,000 varieties of fruits and other crops were tested under harsh prairie conditions.

Beginning in the 1880s, Northern Colorado became a significant fruit growing region, with cherry orchards, in particular, springing up in Loveland and adjacent Masonville. Nearby Fort Collins focused primarily on apples. By the late 1930s, droughts, blight, and devas-tating freezes eventually brought about the end of the region's fruit production. Flying over residential neighborhoods in spring, remnants of the orchards can still be seen scattered throughout the area.

The Dust Bowl of 1930–1936, and the Great Depression from 1929–1933, followed by a recession, all took a toll on the area's farming economy. The Loveland sugar factory continued to operate until 1985 when the Great Western Sugar Co. went bankrupt, and the Loveland plant was closed.

Following World War II, returning servicemen and women were eager to put the past behind them, and a period of economic growth began. The GI bill helped make homeownership possible, and cars allowed householders to work in urban areas and live in the rapidly growing suburbs. Along with post-war prosperity came an explosion of population growth.

Due to increased mechanization, fewer people were needed to operate farms. America's rural population remained virtually the same between 1900 and 2000. However, the population in metropolitan areas (urban and suburban) increased by 203.1 million people over the course of the twentieth century.

One after another, farms were sold for development. The retirement plan for the aging demographic of farm owners became the sale of the family homestead. One result of suburban sprawl is that people now live increasingly far away from their food source, a trend that has been a focus of the local foods movement. Another result of sprawl is that the "human footprint" of non-native vegetation and impermeable surfaces, such as pavement and rooftops, has dramatically reduced the area available for wildlife habitat.

In the book, *Bringing Nature Home,* published in 2009, Douglas Tallamy points out that pavement covers almost 42 million acres in the US and turfgrass covers 40 million acres. He further reveals that 98 percent of the Lower Forty-eight states has been altered for human use.

Here in Colorado, a region that typically gets 12–14 inches of precipitation per year, the average person uses 150 gallons of water per day. Sixty percent of residential water consumption goes to support landscaping. This amounts to approximately 90 gallons of water per person per day used to keep exotic landscapes on life support. Colorado's population in 1900 was 543,000. By 2019, the population had

Suburban sprawl

increased over tenfold to 5.7 million. Over the next twenty years, Colorado's population is expected to grow by roughly 30 percent, increasing from 5.7 million in 2019 to 7.52 million in 2040.

All over the West, landowners, municipalities, developers, and others are looking for strategies to procure water for their own needs. A strategy has developed in some places to "buy and dry" farms, purchasing large sections of land, and stripping off the water rights. Some counties have made this illegal unless, in the process, the abandoned farmland is restored to shortgrass prairie. This type of dry land restoration can be a lengthy and expensive process. In other places, cities have sought to dam or divert rivers. However, none of these practices have the potential for producing more water; they only place a burden on already pressured watersheds.

Runoff from melting snow in the high mountains is the primary water source for much of the Rocky Mountain West. Snow falls in the high country. Wind blows the snow off of the treeless alpine zone. In the subalpine forest below, the snow slowly melts over the summer, and cool streams trickle from the mountains to join the rivers diverted for irrigation and municipal water supplies. Since the supply is dependent on seasonal moisture, it can vary from year to year and diminish as annual heat indices increase.

Global climate change is already impacting the timing and amount of water available in the state. Rising temperatures can lead to fewer but more-intense precipitation events and can alter the ways in which plants grow. The transpiration process of plants pulls water from the soil and disperses it into the atmosphere. Transpiration increases as temperatures warm, which causes the plants to use more water and further dries out the soil. In the summer of 2020, fires burned all over the Rocky Mountain West, particularly in the upper montane and subalpine forests. A changing climate could potentially impede these forest's ability to re-establish themselves.

Although our growing population and a changing climate will reduce available water, thus far, we have made virtually no effort to conserve water in landscaping. However, the rising cost of water is beginning to change how municipalities, developers, and landscape designers are re-envisioning "regionally appropriate landscapes" that utilize native plants adapted to our high altitude, bright sun, and dry climate.

Those who already own a home may support the idea of limiting growth and development. Those who do not own a home, particularly younger people or people living in the developing world, will be drawn to the highest standard of living achievable. The question though is not "to grow or not to grow?" Instead, we ask how growth can be sustainable, equitable, and compatible with the goals of environmental stewardship and ultimately our survival.

Before we move on, some people will say economic growth cannot continue endlessly without natural systems, like our water supply, collapsing. This is true; a carrying capacity imposes limits on growth, which must be considered. However, we have only begun to scratch the surface of sustainable growth that contributes to environmental restoration. This is the focus of the High Plains Environmental Center.

CHAPTER 4

NEW BEGINNINGS ON AN OLD HOMESTEAD

I n the late 1990s, Chad and Troy McWhinney, founders of their namesake real estate investment and development company, brought their plans for a 3,000-acre master-planned development to the City Planning Department in Loveland, Colorado. The land, now known as Centerra, sits in an area described as an economic center for development in Northern Colorado. Interstate 25 runs through the land from north to south, and Colorado Highway 34 lies adjacent to the property's southern edge.

A portion of the land had belonged to the McWhinney's great-grandfather, John Hahn, who claimed the homestead in 1860. The remainder was purchased from various owners. The land was primarily actively farmed or abandoned farmland. A junkyard containing an entire railroad car sat on the westernmost portion of the land.

The City's response to McWhinney's proposal included a stipulation that the land would be 20 percent open space at buildout. Open space, in this context, refers to parks, stormwater ponds, and natural areas. McWhinney hired a group called Cedar Creek to conduct an environmental assessment to identify "environmentally sensitive areas."

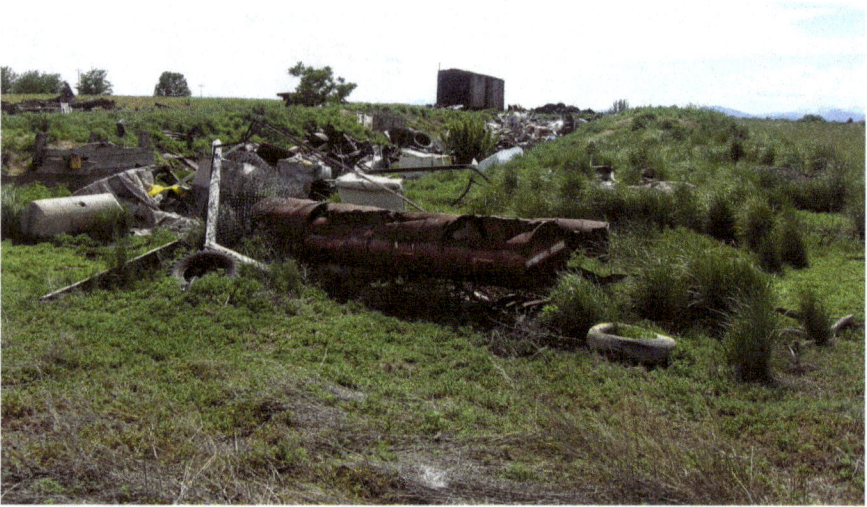

An old farm dump west of Houts Reservoir contained a whole railroad car

An ocean of weeds, Canada thistle (*Cirsium arvense*)

The Cedar Creek study of 1999 clearly reflected the history of the land by evaluating its present state, which was basically an ocean of weeds with faint reminders of a former shortgrass prairie environment. It read as follows:

This nearly level development parcel is composed of actively cultivated cropland and two irrigation reservoirs, Houts Reservoir and Equalizer Lake, as well as wetland, disturbed/weedy grasslands and rabbitbrush grassland habitats. Cropland, disturbed weedy areas, and rabbitbrush grassland do not meet any criteria for classification of environmentally sensitive areas. Cropland is seasonally disturbed and lacking vegetation cover between late fall and spring. It provides minimal wildlife habitat except for occasional foraging by Canada geese after harvest.

Disturbed weedy areas have been cleared of vegetation and revegetated by primarily weedy and non-native grasses and forbs. Dominant vegetation in these areas included kochia (*Kochia scoparia*) prickly lettuce (*Lactuca serriola*) flixweed (*Descurainia sophia*) Canada thistle (*Cirsium arvense*), intermediate wheatgrass (*Agropyron intermedium*), western wheatgrass (*Agropyron smithii*), cheatgrass (*Bromus tectorum*).

The disturbed weedy area on the West side of Houts Reservoir also contained scattered trash, piles of old car bodies, and abandoned farm implements, particularly at the South end. The two rabbitbrush grassland habitat parcels on the West side of Equalizer Lake appeared to have had some surface disturbance in the past and currently support a mixture of native shrubs and non-native weedy species. Dominant vegetation in this habitat was rabbitbrush (*Chrysothamnus nauseosus*), fringed sage (*Artemisia frigida*), broom snakeweed (*Gutierrezia sarothrae*), winterfat (*Kraschenninnikovia lanata*), crested wheatgrass (*Agropyron cristatum*) cheatgrass, kochia, and Russian thistle (*Salsola kali*).

An abundance of migratory waterfowl at HPEC includes ducks such as northern shovelers.

The Cedar Creek report evaluated areas surrounding two reservoirs (Houts Reservoir and Equalizer Lake) and suggested setbacks based on existing habitat value. Because the land surrounding Houts was farmed extensively, the habitat value was lower, and the minimal setbacks were 75 feet from the shoreline. The areas surrounding Equalizer were not farmed and preserved some remnant prairie vegetation. The largest recommended setback for this area was 300 feet from the shoreline. The reservoirs, dug nearly 100 years earlier, had become particularly valuable habitat for migratory waterfowl.

In addition to the areas around the reservoir, a natural watershed and cottonwood grove spanning approximately forty-four acres was identified on the east side of Centerra. This area would later become the Chapungu Sculpture Park. Other areas that would ultimately make up the approximate 600-acre open space include stormwater ponds and restored grassland owned by the Centerra Metropolitan District.

McWhinney partnered with McStain Neighborhoods, a residential home builder, which led to the creation of High Plains Village, a residential development that utilized a model of high density inter-spersed with pocket parks and open space. Tom Hoyt, the president of McStain, was both a developer and conservationist. He said, "You can't talk about one without the other, they go hand in hand."

At HPEC we believe that when planning and development are tak-ing place, that is where habitat can be preserved, even created. Nature can and must be a stakeholder. For nature and wildlife to have a voice at the table, Tom suggested creating a 501(c)3 nonprofit to own the conservation land surrounding Houts and Equalizer. On March 21st, the first day of spring in 2001, the High Plains Environmental Center (HPEC) was born.

The developers, McStain and McWhinney, committed to donating seventy-six acres surrounding the reservoirs to be owned and managed by the Environmental Center. An agreement with the Greeley Love-land Irrigation Company (GLIC) secured a perpetual lease for the lake surface rights for the Environmental Center. The surface lease with the GLIC is directly tied to residential development within the High Plains Village and Lakes at Centerra Neighborhoods. The cost is based on how many homes are built. The developers voluntarily imposed an en-vironmental assessment fee to be collected by the city during the per-mitting process for all projects within Centerra, west of the interstate. The fee is based on square footage and zoning of the project (residen-tial, office, or commercial). They also imposed a "transfer fee" on the sale of residential properties in perpetuity to help fund operations and capital projects at HPEC and help fund the annual lease on the surface rights of the two lakes.

Through HPEC's agreement with GLIC, residents are allowed ac-cess for non-motorized boats to the northern lake, Houts Reservoir, within a prescribed season, intended to minimize impact on the spring and fall waterfowl migration on the lake. The southern reservoir, Equal-izer Lake, is exclusively reserved for wildlife, and no surface water use is permitted. The setbacks around these lakes produce dramatically dif-ferent results than the neighborhoods that allow lots with mowed turf grass to extend all the way to the water's edge.

One distinctive difference in Centerra is that we have far less algae than typical lakes within a residential development. The unmown native vegetation (shrubs, grasses, and wetland plants) in the setbacks and stormwater conveyances function as a biological filter, helping to sequester nutrient runoff from adjacent developed sites. The proof of our strategy's environmental success is measured and proven in periodic water quality testing and counts of fish and wildlife conducted by Colorado Parks and Wildlife and Front Range Community College.

From its inception, this model has not only avoided the all-too-common opposition of business versus environment, it has created a partnership that is beneficial to commerce, conservation, and community. The developer heavily markets the nature component of the master planned community with taglines such as "nature in your backyard" and "enjoy a healthy outdoor lifestyle."

After HPEC helped Centerra earn certification as the first Wildlife Habitat Community in the state of Colorado by the National Wildlife Federation, "Certified Wild" has been used to advertise Centerra.

From the perspective of the Environmental Center, this kind of promotion seems very likely to attract a demographic that resonates with our vision: people who are interested in volunteering for conservation projects, participating in citizen science, birding, and attending classes on gardening with native plants.

The relationship between the community, the developer, and the environmental center is by no means without challenges. However, the interweaving of planning, development, marketing, community engagement, and conservation funding are embedded in the model where the need to work together is much stronger than the impulse to drift apart.

The HPEC holds a permanent seat on the Centerra Design Review Committee which reviews every architectural and landscape design within Centerra. In this capacity, HPEC is afforded the opportunity to reject inappropriate or potentially invasive plant material, make suggestions and inject ideas at formative stages of the design process that help the community best reflect its partnership with HPEC. The design review process safeguards the quality, style, and cohesiveness of the horticulture and the overall appearance of the development.

Funding for such an endeavor has presented its own challenges. The funds derived from the environmental assessment fees were

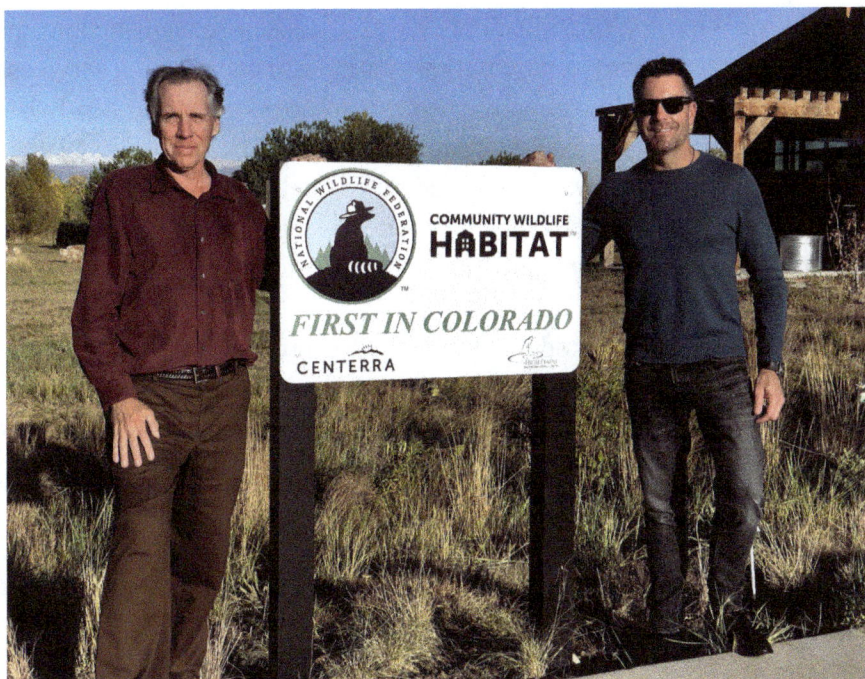

Jim Tolstrup and Chad McWhinney

anticipated to grow much faster than they actually did. The original funding agreement timed out in 2020 and thankfully, working together with the developer, and the agreement has been extended to 2040. Virtually no fees were generated during the recession of 2011–2013. As a result of slower growth, the fund did not increase sufficiently to yield earnings and interest to meet the cost of land management obligations transferred to HPEC.

Before 2008, HPEC had virtually no revenue source other than the environmental assessment fees. HPEC functioned by consuming the fees as operating revenue. The HPEC board of directors were very intent on making the land a leading-edge example of environmental restoration and stewardship. In 2008, HPEC purchased equipment and hired staff to manage our own land, as well as offering land management services to the developer and landowners within Centerra and other communities along the Front Range.

With HPEC's help, leadership in environmental stewardship and restoration has become a distinguishing characteristic of Centerra, and for the McWhinney organization as well. Mission-related income in the form of fees for environmental restoration and consultation services has allowed HPEC educational programs to operate independently of revenue generated by the environmental fees. This has allowed the fees to function as they were intended: to fuel the growth of an endowment that would help to underwrite the cost of maintaining the seventy-six-acre park, and safeguard the long-term mission and goals of the organization.

With this financial model in place, HPEC built a public visitor center in 2017 at the cost of $1.2 million, with additional support from McWhinney and the City of Loveland. The HPEC endowment grew to $1.5 million in 2021.

CHAPTER 5

WHAT WE BUILT AND WHY

Early in the project, McWhinney and McStain removed old cars buried on the lakeshore by farmers to slow erosion. The developers stabilized the banks with rocks, and a subsequent volunteer project covered up much of this rock by planting 1,000 native trees and shrubs. This created a habitat for kingfishers, a bird that perches over water to hunt minnows, and it improved fish habitat by providing cover for insects. The layer of shrubs and trees on the north side of the environmental center site helped cut cold winds coming off the lake, which improved the site for horticulture.

The developers built a four-mile trail around the two lakes, taking care to avoid the higher value habitat areas. A park was built, which included a gazebo, concrete walkways, and irrigated landscaping. The park was named Old Canal Park because it was built on an island between an irrigation ditch abandoned in 1907 and Equalizer Lake, a reservoir that was created the same year.

A series of stormwater ponds will be created by the developer on HPEC land. This is an excellent arrangement for both parties because it gets the ponds off the buildable lots and places high-value habitat restoration on HPEC land. The ponds also serve to "polish" the stormwater that would otherwise flow directly into the reservoirs.

Shoreline stabilization (Photo: HPEC Archive)

Barn and pumpkin patch

Owl cam

The Barn

In 2006, the developers moved a circa 1900 horse barn across Interstate Highway 25 to the HPEC property. The barn was the first thing to be placed on the site and sat for two years in an alfalfa field at the trail's edge. In 2007, a group of community volunteers painted the barn. At the same time, a nesting box was mounted in the rafters of the barn for barn owls. Owls have occupied the barn since spring 2008. Banding the owls has contributed to scientific research, and we have learned that our owls are not always the same pair. In 2012, a camera was added to the nesting box to provide additional data.

Colorado Avian Research and Rehabilitation Institute (CARRI) hosts the owl cam, which has been watched by thousands of people from as far away as Australia. Since there was no electric power at the barn, HPEC staff built a solar-powered system to drive the owl cam. Besides serving as a home to the owls, the barn functions primarily as

Early vegetable garden

tool storage and provides an excellent backdrop to the adjacent community garden.

Until 2015, the HPEC site was difficult to access. It was a mile down a dirt road that became impassable when it rained. A "no trespassing" sign at the paved road kept most visitors at bay. A four-acre site that would become the visitor center and demonstration gardens was carved out of the alfalfa field. For ten years, the site functioned primarily as a vegetable garden. Pumpkins were grown and distributed to area schools, and produce harvested for donation to local food banks.

Community Gardens

Community garden plots were one of the first things created on the site. In 2017, the community garden was substantially reorganized. A total of ninety-two raised beds were installed with the help of volunteers. Individuals can sign up for the boxes and are responsible for watering,

Community garden

caring for, and cleaning out the boxes at the end of the season. The community garden creates its own culture of camaraderie and cooperation. Community members meet their fellow gardeners, share garden produce, and cover for each other when one is going out of town and needs help watering.

Native Plant Nursery

The Native Plant Nursery is the heart of what we do at HPEC, and the program for which we are the most widely known. We promote the use of native plants because they are adapted to our climate, help to conserve water, and provide essential forage for pollinators. We have often heard from people who want to grow native plants in their gardens but can't find them in local nurseries. We began our native plant propagation by hiking and collecting seed, much of it at the Shambhala Mountain Center in Red Feather Lakes, Colorado.

Children visiting the Community Garden can dig in and play in the sensory garden while their parents tend garden plots.

Seed collected locally can often be better than seed from other areas. While not a separate species, locally collected seeds may be a unique genotype adapted to specific conditions. Many ecologists focus on seed genotypes when doing restoration work and will not use seed from differing altitudes or locations. Each year the HPEC nursery produces plants of more than 100 species, many from seeds harvested around our own property. The nursery functions as a school by providing hands-on instruction for students of all ages. Proceeds from the nursery help to cover the cost of educational outreach and the maintenance of demonstration gardens.

Demonstration Gardens Showcase Native Plants

The grounds surrounding our visitor center are entirely vegetated with native plants, many of which have been grown in our nursery from wild-collected seed. The gardens are a living seed bank, where seeds are collected for propagation in the nursery and use in restoration projects.

The nursery at HPEC produces over 150 species of Prairie and Rocky Mountain plants.

We have learned that in drought years, very little seed may be produced in the wild, and many of these seeds cannot be purchased anywhere, making collection from our own gardens all the more valuable.

Our main garden, which we call the Promenade, is a long rectangular bed that aligns with the barn. The centerline of the promenade garden is the main axis of the entire site, and every other feature is measured off of this line. The garden began in 2015 with a large volunteer project that planted hedges and shrubs.

The original concept was to create a sort of "shruboretum" since we didn't have a large-enough site for an arboretum. The site contains sixty species of native shrubs and trees and more than 100 species of native grasses and wildflowers. The gardens on our site have helped us develop a horticulture style in which we virtually never water after establishment and allow a natural succession of plants to coexist within plant communities.

We rely on volunteers to manage weeds, which diminished as the garden has established. We use no insecticides. Our succession of bloom, from April through October, supports a thriving population of

Early garden planting with Volunteers for Outdoor Colorado

Promenade garden: desert four o'clock (*Mirabilis multiflora*) sacred datura (*Datura wrightii*), maximilian sunflower (*Helianthus Maximiliani*) Rocky Mountain bee plant (*Cleome serrulata*)

pollinators, and the gardens fill with bird songs throughout the year. Our gardens are free and open to the public. Our gardening style and ethic are explored in greater detail in Section II.

Seed Shed

The seed shed is the most recent addition to our site. It has helped alleviate the chaos caused by having piles of drying plants and seeds being cleaned all over our office. It is not ideal to keep seeds in a temperature-controlled environment where lots of people breathe moisture into the air. Seeds ideally are kept dry and cool. When summer comes, we move our cleaned and packaged seeds into our barn to keep them cool. The work that we do is called "ex-situ conservation." It's not preserving an intact natural area, it's introducing species into a restored area or landscape. As our friend Mike Bone at Denver Botanic Gardens says, "Propagation is conservation."

Seed shed

Wild Zone

Many of us grew up in places and a time, where we were allowed to wander freely and play in nature. Many children either don't have the space or the inclination to be. In 2007, Richard Louve wrote *The Last Child in the Woods*, a groundbreaking work on children and nature. Louve postulates that children require time for unstructured play in nature for healthy development and links the epidemic of ADD/ADHD to what he terms "nature deficit disorder."

The Wild Zone is a response to this concept of intentionally allowing children the space to connect with nature. A Wild Zone can be virtually any natural outdoor space where kids can play. It can be highly developed or completely undeveloped. The basic idea is to allow kids to interact with nature in a not excessively sanitized or scripted setting.

Maria Montessori said that "play is the work of the child." Play is where children literally build their brains and develop critical thinking, creativity, and resourcefulness. The Wild Zone at HPEC is simply an area set aside with climbing logs and a rock pile. Sections of wood have been left out where kids can use them to construct tipis, forts, and musical instruments. We've seen children create drawings and craft projects and tie them to trees. With so many rules in place in natural areas (for good reasons), the Wild Zone is a place with minimal barriers to connecting with nature.

In 2016–2017, we built a visitors' center and office for HPEC. The 2,450 square foot building is compact but highly functional, with a high standard of aesthetic details.

The building includes a classroom for programs and visiting students and a kitchen and bathrooms for program support. A board member, Ken Morgan, who was, until recently, a wildlife biologist with Colorado Parks and Wildlife, helped us build a collection of taxidermized bird specimens and other artifacts in our small but well-stocked library.

The best feature of our center is its proximity to the work that we do. From our classroom, our mission can be observed in neighborhood open space, gardens filled with native plants, stormwater ponds, and wildlife. A kestrel nest box with a video camera on top of our roof allows us to watch these birds breeding and rearing their young.

Wild Zone

Every child deserves access to nature

Visitor Center

HPEC library and wildlife specimens

Native Landscaping at HPEC. Mass plantings such as this Palmer's penstemon (*Penstemon palmeri*) can be highly impactful if you have the space but the effect can be short term. For this reason, most residential gardens utilize smaller and more diverse groupings.

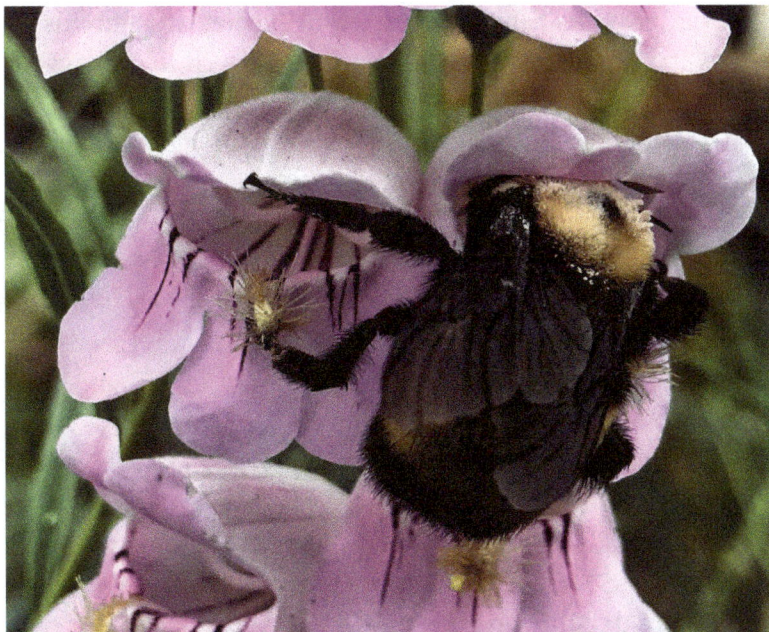

Palmer's penstemon (*Penstemon palmeri*) is visited by bumblebees when the queens emerge from the ground in springtime.

Chapungu

In addition to our gardens, we have created extensive water-conserving gardens at the Chapungu Sculpture Park. This 26-acre site was one of the areas of habitat value identified in the Cedar Creek Study in 1999. The entire site is a watershed with many large old cottonwood trees. The GLIC canal bisects the park. The northern part of the park is more intensively landscaped and is the part of the park with more activities, concerts, gatherings, and displays of holiday lights.

The southern two-thirds of the park are a wooded natural area with a walking trail and some intensively managed garden areas. The south end of the park has a large natural pond that remains full year-round. Water from this pond flows under a bridge into a sixteen-acre woodland below. This is an entirely undeveloped natural area with a cottonwood grove and an extensive understory of native shrubs. Preserving urban forests such as this helps to sequester carbon, reduces the "urban heat island," and preserves local genotypes in the case of wild shrubs and trees.

The park provides habitat for numerous species of songbirds. Hummingbirds are commonly seen in summer, as well as turkeys and at least two active raptor nests. Many of the old cottonwood trees host hives of feral European honeybees. Native pollinators are abundant, particularly since many native plants have been planted.

The name Chapungu refers to the Bateleur eagle, the emblem of Zimbabwe, in the language of the Shona people. Zimbabwean stone sculpture has become known worldwide. The park hosts more than eighty examples of this work, grouped in themes representing traditional Shona values, women, children, the family, elders, and the spirit world.

Kim Perry, vice president of Community Design at McWhinney, met Roy Guthrie and Marcey Mushore, who were curating a sculpture collection that had traveled internationally to botanic gardens. Roy and Marcey were seeking a place where the collection could be permanently housed. Following this meeting, arrangements were made to bring the sculptures to Centerra as a permanent exhibit. The collection

Chapungu trail

Chapungu, Sky Pond Drive bridge

Prince's plume (*Stanleya pinnata*) and two-tailed swallowtail

Chapungu refers to the bateleur eagle, the emblem of Zimbabwe

Agastache 'Blue Fortune' and brown-belted bumblebee

now resides at Chapungu Sculpture Park, which is free and open to the public year-round.

The park landscape was designed by DTJ Design, an international landscape architecture, building architecture, and land planning firm with offices in Boulder, Austin, and Atlanta. The park was built in 2007 and 2008. HPEC took over management of the park in 2009. Over time, as the original plantings declined, HPEC redesigned the beds with an increased focus on water conservation and the use of native plants.

Many of the new plantings in the park focus on the Plant Select palette. Plant Select is a collaboration between Denver Botanic Gardens, Colorado State University, and professional horticulturists. The program's focus is to introduce plants for landscaping (native or non-native) that are well-adapted to Colorado's high and dry climate. We also included many of the favorite native plants we grow in our nursery.

The gardens at Chapungu are intended to be showy and support pollinators. They are also experimental; it's a place where we have

Chapungu beds designed by Jim Tolstrup and J.R. Oldham include azure sage (*Salvia azurea*), Joe-Pye weed (*Eutrochium purpureum*), West Texas grass sage (*Salvia reptans*), baby blue rabbitbrush (*Chrysothamnus nauseosus var. nauseosus*) 'Thin Man' Indiangrass (*Sorghastrum nutans "Thin Man*), and agastache "Blue Fortune".

Chapungu beds designed by Jim Tolstrup and J.R. Oldham. Azure sage (*Salvia azurea*), Joe-Pye weed (*Eutrochium purpurea*), chocolate flower (*Berlandiera lyrata*), California poppy (*Eschscholzia californica*), *Penstemon x mexicali Red Rocks*, sunset hyssop (*Agastache rupestris*), *Agastache aurantiaca 'Coronado'*.

Plant Select beds include salvia greggii 'Furman's red', sunset hyssop (*Agastache rupestris*), VALLEY LAVENDER® (*Verbena bipinnatifida*), hummingbird trumpet (*Epilobium canum ssp. garrettii*), 'Blonde Ambition' blue grama grass (*Bouteloua gracilis*), regal torch lily (*Kniphofia caulescens*), CORONADO® hyssop (*Agastache aurantiaca*)

pushed the envelope of plants used within Centerra as a whole. Many plants that were planted in Chapungu first are now being used elsewhere within the development. Chapungu, like the best of public gardens, is experimental and educational.

In 2020, we began an experiment testing the impacts of road salts on various grass species at Chapungu. A series of test plots along the road on the outer border of Chapungu include native grass, turf grasses, and common ornamental grasses growing side by side. The resulting data will be posted on our website. The grasses being tested include the following, with Colorado native grasses denoted with an (n):

Alkali sacaton. *Sporobolus airoides* (n)

Blue grama grass. *Bouteloua gracilis* (n)

Buffalo grass. *Buchloe dactyloides* (n)

Dog Tuff grass. *Cynodon hybrida 'Dog Tuff'*

Grass test plots

Fountain grass. *Pennisetum alopecuroides*

Karl Foerster grass. *Calamagrostis x acutiflora 'Karl Foerster'*

Kentucky bluegrass. *Poa pratensis*

Little bluestem. *Schizachyrium scoparium* (n)

Saltgrass. *Distichlis spicata* (n)

Slender wheatgrass. *Elymus trachycaulus* (n)

Tall fescue. *Festuca arundinacea*

Western wheatgrass. *Pascopyrum smithii* (n)

CHAPTER 6

A GARDEN OF RECONCILIATION

Powwow for third-graders

For many years, HPEC has hosted a mini powwow for third graders from the Thompson School District in Loveland. The educational unit for third grade includes study of Native American history and culture. A Native American group, the Iron Family of Fort Collins, has been invited to share their culture with the students. The Iron Family performs traditional songs and dances in full regalia. At the end of the presentation, the students are invited to participate in a round dance together. The awkwardness and joy of the dance always produces smiles and giggles in children and adults, and remind us of our shared humanity.

Once, during a gathering near Halloween, Jan Iron told the students that she hates to see pumpkins smashed in the street. You should offer that pumpkin back to the earth and the animals and say, "Thank you for bringing me some happiness." It was a mind-blowing transmission of indigenous culture that they could never have gotten from reading a book.

In 2018 and 2019, Volunteers for Outdoor Colorado helped us build a suitable and permanent place to host events showcasing indigenous culture. The Medicine Wheel Garden consists of an inner dance circle, 60 feet across, surrounded by a double circle of posts that create a shade arbor when wild grapes grow to cover them. This is a traditional configuration for ceremonial and social dance grounds. Outside of the arbor, raised beds contain plants used for food, ceremony, and medicine by tribes of the High Plains. Each plant is labeled with scientific, common, and Lakota names.

Indigenous Medicine

If a native person shows you a medicinal plant, he or she may well admonish, "Don't tell anyone." It's not that they are greedy or selfish. Quite the opposite; in native cultures, people will often endure hunger and thirst and shed their life's blood for the benefit of the others. The protection of this information is rather because native people know how our materialistic culture works, that everything is for sale, and everything is subject to exploitation.

The relationship to plants in Native American culture is vastly different from Euro-American culture. When a traditional native person is looking for a plant, they may sit down by the first one they find and offer tobacco. They might pray and ask permission to take the plant, and that it may bring healing. Then one might begin to notice that these little plants are all around. Relating to plants this way is a matter of acknowledgment and respect that comes from a perspective of humility,

Iron Family

gratitude, and relationship—the foundation of healing in traditional native culture.

From the indigenous perspective, not acknowledging plants as relatives reduces them to "things" to be used rather than beings that contain their own wisdom and power. For this reason, only having the ability to identify plants is not enough. In native cultures, it's not the plants alone that can heal people but the qualities of the person administering them and the sacred context of ceremony.

Due to the concerns about this knowledge being exploited, native people have been protective of it. Therefore, many scholars have traveled to Indian reservations and concluded that the knowledge and uses of plants had been lost. However, knowledge is there waiting to be discovered by those who can see, as the Lakota say, with the *čanté ištá* (*Chan-tay Eesh-tah*), "the eyes of the heart."

The knowledge of plant uses among Native Americans came from experimentation and insight and has been transmitted from person to person in a long oral history. Euro-Americans have benefited from the

Curlycup gumweed (*Grindelia squarrosa*)

knowledge of plants accumulated by Native Americans as in the case of Joe Pye, an Indian who used the plant named after him, Joe Pye weed (*Eutrochium purpureum*) to cure a typhoid outbreak in colonial Massachusetts.

John Neihardt's hauntingly poetic *Black Elk Speaks*, about an Oglala holy man's life, provides an example of the knowledge of plants through spiritual insight. In a vision, Black Elk saw a particular plant being used to cure illness. Later he and his friend, One Side, sit on a hill, watching hawks circle a spot nearby, and he says, "I believe that yonder grows the plant from my vision." They ride over to the spot and, "There right on the side of the bank the herb was growing, and I knew it, although I had never seen one like it before except in my vision."

In the Lakota language, plants are often named for where they are found, how they are used, or their distinguishing characteristics. *Artemisia ludoviciana*, prairie sage is called *pȟežíhóta* (*pay-zhee ho-tah*), "something gray in the grass." This plant is used for purification. *Artemisia tridentata*, big sagebrush, is *pȟežíhóta tȟáŋka* (*pay-zhee ho-tah taan-kah*), which means the same as above but bigger.

Asclepias pumila, low milkweed, is *čhešlóšlo pȟežúta*, (*Chay-shlo-shlo Pay-zhoo-tah*), which means diarrhea medicine. *Galium boreale*, northern bedstraw, is *čhaŋȟlóǧaŋ ská waštémna* (*chan-hlo-gan washtay mana*), which is traditionally worn under the belts of Lakota women as a sashay. The name means "good white herb" because of its wholesome hay-scented fragrance and white flowers.

Before there were drugstores and supermarkets, people had to find food, medicine, and everything they needed in nature. Doing that required a tremendous amount of knowledge about plants and animals, the various ecological zones, where things grew, and about phenology: the study of periodic plant and animal life cycle events and how these are influenced by seasonal and interannual variations in climate as well as habitat factors like elevation.

Timing is critically important when harvesting plants for food and medicine. Plants such as milkweed can be beneficial at some times and may be toxic at others. Many edible plants are easily confused with poisonous ones, and medicinal plants can be harmful in excessive or improperly prepared doses.

We do not intend that anyone harvest or use these plants. Many plant species have been over-collected, depleting wild populations. The reference to wild plants' uses here is strictly for educational purposes and should not be used as a practical guide.

There are also ceremonial reasons connected with harvesting plants. Green ash, (*Fraxinus pennsylvanica*) or *psehtíŋ čháŋ* (*psay-ha-teen cha*), are used for pipe stems because of their pithy core that can be burned out easily. It is said that trees are protected by the Thunder Beings, *Wakiŋyaŋ Oyáte* (*wah-ki-yang oh-yah-tay*), and ash stems can only be cut in winter, before thunder. Stems cut in springtime, after thunder returns, will crack.

Some particularly valuable and efficacious plants were (and are) gathered, dried, and stored. Others are simply gathered and utilized as needed and as available. People traveling through different types of terrain could find plants for various common ailments, as well as food, wherever they went and in any season.

Many native plants that may be growing in our gardens have traditional uses. *Liatris punctata*, or dotted blazing star, has been

When there was no drugstore

used to help stimulate appetite. Its Lakota name, *tatéte čhaŋnúŋǧa* (*tah-tay-tay cha-nung-gah*), means that it faces the four directions. Echinacea (particularly *E. angustifolia*) is used for toothaches. Its Lakota name, *uŋglákčapi* (*oong-glak-chapi*), indicates that the dried flowers are something you can "comb your hair with." The word for common sunflowers (*Helianthus annuus*), *waȟčá zizí*, (*wah-cha ghee-ghee*) means a "very yellow flower." These can be boiled to extract oil to soften the skin.

It has been said that when the languages of indigenous people disappear, their environments collapse. There is an ethic and a world view encoded in the language. Knowing the ancient names of these plants provides a window into the primordial prairies. We will never heal and restore the lands of the Western hemisphere until we come to a place of reconciliation with its original inhabitants.

In 2019, HPEC hosted the Lakota Reconciliation Ride on horseback, which begins in Sedalia, Colorado, and spans 400 miles, ending

Tipi Raisers hoop dance

at the Pine Ridge Reservation in South Dakota. The ride is intended to bring awareness and support to the self-sufficiency projects that the host organization, the Tipi Raisers, supports on the reservation. The ride is also a reconciliation, a mission to create goodwill and understanding between the native riders and the Front Range communities they visit.

CHAPTER 7

PRESERVING AN AGRICULTURAL LEGACY

Heirloom apples

W e planted an heirloom fruit orchard at HPEC to preserve a portion of the region's agricultural heritage. The orchard includes apples, cherries, plums, peaches, and raspberries. From the late 1800s until the 1930s, Northern Colorado was a fruit-growing area. The USDA-ARS field station in Cheyenne, Wyoming, tested over 5,000 varieties of fruits between 1929 and 1974. All but fifty of the trees were destroyed, and water was cut off in 1974 when the field station's focus shifted from horticulture to grazing animal management, mining reclamation, and water conservation.

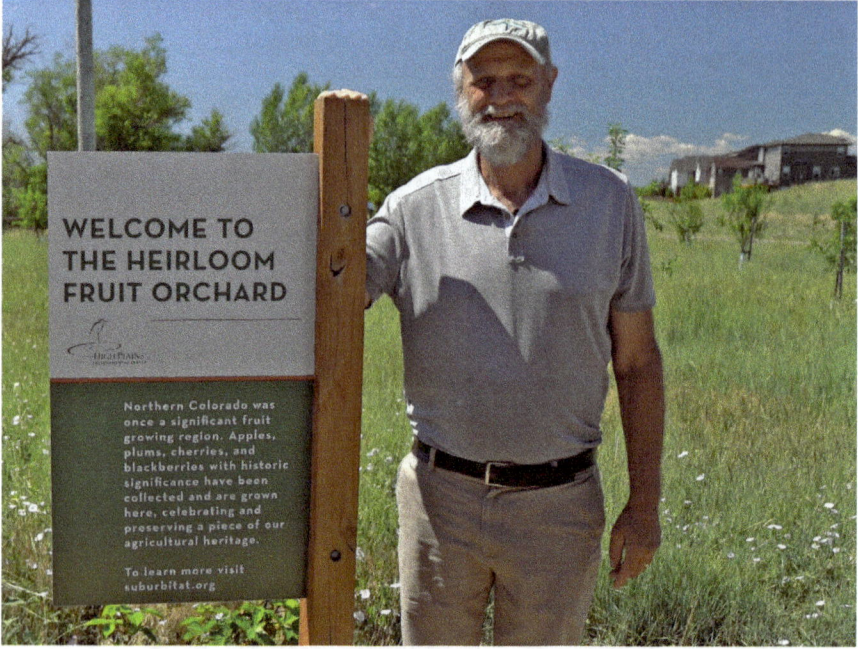

Scott Skogerboe (Photo Credit: Nick Clement)

Our friend, Scott Skogerboe, a highly skilled woody plant propagator at Fort Collins Wholesale Nursery, discovered how to get many native shrubs to grow from seed and helped to make these plants available for Colorado horticulture. Scott has also spent his life collecting apple varieties that were once grown locally and many other varieties of historical interest. Many of these trees have found a home in our heirloom fruit orchard at HPEC. We interviewed Scott to get the back story on some of these apple varieties.

Haas. In 1892, the *Fort Collins Courier* newspaper asked Charles Pennock, a pioneer orchardist and nurseryman, which varieties he recommended for Larimer County. At the top of his list for commercial production was Haas. Scott says, "I could see why Charles Pennock named that variety, it was crisp, it was juicy, it had just enough sweetness to subacid balance. The skin on it is glossy and beautiful, red all the way around, except for a small green part on the shady side of the apple."

One of the reasons this variety may have died out is that modern apple varieties have names conducive to marketing, like Red Delicious and Honeycrisp. The Haas (meaning "rabbit" in German) was found on the Gabriel Cerre estate in St Louis, the present-day location of The Gateway Arch in St Louis. I don't know who it was named after. I suspect it was probably just named after a person with that surname who gave it to Mr. Cerre.

Wealthy. Another apple on Charles Pennock's list was called "Wealthy." It was the first apple released by Peter Gideon of the University of Minnesota in 1880. Gideon tried to find apples that could survive in Minnesota because European apple varieties would not survive Minnesota's 30–40 below zero temperatures. Gideon crossed cold-hardy Siberian crabapples with edible apples.

Utter's Red. This variety was also on Charles Pennock's list in 1892. It was another commercially grown apple from Wisconsin.

Goodhue. This was one of the top-ten apples at the Cheyenne Station. It came from Goodhue County, Minnesota, from an amateur fruit breeder named T.R. Perkins. Goodhue rose to the top of the 5,000 varieties tested at Cheyenne.

Gravenstein. Scott says, "Gravenstein is one of my personal favorites. Prior to getting my degree in horticulture, I was in the army and stationed in San Francisco. In Sonoma County, there's a highway called the Gravenstein Highway. That's where this Danish apple, the Gravenstein, is at its finest. Every year when the apples were ripe local grocery stores would fill with Gravensteins, and man, when you have a freshly picked Gravenstein, you want to have it in your yard. It's such a delicious apple."

Maiden Blush. Scott describes an old farm in Fort Collins that was knocked down in the '70s and apartment complexes built in its place. "If there was an apple tree that didn't fall where there was going to be a parking lot or an apartment building, they just left it. I drove by there one day and saw this apple tree loaded with yellow apples with a pink edge on the sunny side and man that was such a good apple, so I went, and I propagated it, and I didn't really know what it was and so this is really just an educated guess I believe it was maiden blush, judging by the size of the tree and the apples that were around 100 years ago."

Colorado Orange. The Colorado Orange Apple was developed in Colorado and was grown in other Western states until it fell into obscurity. It was rediscovered by Jude and Addie Schuenemeyer, who run the Montezuma Orchard Restoration Project, a nonprofit that rescues heirloom varieties, in Cortez, Colorado.

Renown. The Renown apple is still alive at the Cheyenne Station, forty-six years after the irrigation was turned off. The tree came from the Agriculture Canada Research Station in Indian Head, Saskatchewan. Ag Canada started breeding plants and testing plants at all these horticulture stations and did the same thing that Peter Gideon had done in Minnesota. They crossed hardy crabapples with edible apples in the hopes of coming up with something that would survive the winter on the Canadian prairie. The Renown apple was one of them.

In Indianhead, there was an orphanage where children were often left during the Great Depression to be cared for while their parents looked for work. The orphans would often visit the Ag Station. One day, the station director watched kids going from tree to tree tasting the apples. They'd take a bite, and if the apple was no good and they'd throw it away. If they liked it, they'd fill their pockets. One of the children started jumping up and calling to his friends. All the orphans went over to this one tree, each one that tasted the fruit, emptied their pockets of all the other apples, and filled them up with this one. It was just a numbered selection, and it didn't have a name, so they named it Renown.

The Flower of Kent. The Flower of Kent was Isaac Newton's apple that gave him the idea of the law of gravity. In 1665, there was a pandemic during which the black death swept through Europe. They closed the universities and sent the students home, shut the shops, and restricted travel. Young Isaac Newton went home to Woolsthorpe Manor in Grantham, England. There he saw his mother's cooking apple, the Flower of Kent, fall, and it made him wonder why. *What made this object—and all others—fall to earth?* That's where he formulated the idea for the law of gravity. The apple is enormous, and the thud as it struck the earth was probably hard to miss.

Johnny Appleseed. Johnny Appleseed is a character from American folklore based on a real person. He planted apples from seed, which did not reliably produce edible apples. The purpose of the apples was primarily to produce hard cider. Later settlers brought cuttings of edible apple varieties. For this reason, in Ohio and Indiana, where Johnny Appleseed planted his apple seedlings, the trees were later destroyed.

Scott wanted to find more trees with a historical background. "I wanted more trees with a living tie to history, so I started thinking. *Of course, being an American*, I thought, *Johnny Appleseed planted millions of apple trees. Surely someone has to have one of those in their collection.* By 1961, I learned there was only one tree alive, and it was in Ashland, Ohio. It was shown on the front page of the *Cleveland Plain Dealer*. Unfortunately, that tree died in 1965, but the man whose farm it was on was still alive, his name was Roy Funk. I called Mr. Funk, introduced myself, and said I was looking for it, and he said, "Oh, that tree was the pride of our farm. We bought the farm in 1959, and it was alive for a few years after that, but it unfortunately died."

Fortunately, there was a seventh-grader from Brunswick, Ohio, who had asked for a cutting. That seventh grader, now an adult, was a local orchardist by the name of Eyssen, and Scott was able to obtain a cutting from him. Bill Eyssen had kept the original cutting alive by grafting it onto an old Cortland apple near his apple pie bakery.

Scott describes the apples as follows, "It's actually a decent apple.

It's red, it's attractive, it's sweet, it's crisp, it has some juiciness to it, but it's bland. I think if you blended that with other apples, it would make a good cider. Imagine having apple cider made from the last tree of Johnny Appleseed."

Hung Hai Tung. One of the most interesting plants still alive at the USDA Horticulture Station in Cheyenne is the Hung Hai Tung crabapple. It was planted there in 1929, so the tree is now ninety-one years old. For many people who visit this abandoned horticulture station in Cheyenne, it's their favorite tree. It's massive, probably forty feet tall. It has apples about the size of a ping-pong ball that are pretty decent for a crabapple. It has two-inch diameter flowers, which makes the tree ornamentally desirable.

A famous explorer named P.H. Dorset who went to China in 1927 during the Chinese Revolution found refuge at night by sleeping in Buddhist temples. In Central China, he stopped at the temple by the name of Fa Hua Su, which means the Temple of Transformational Thoughts. He learned that when a Buddhist monk died, they put their ashes in the field and planted a tree as living stupas to remember them. Dorset took cuttings from the tree, and some ended up at the Cheyenne Station.

SECTION II

RESTORING NATURE

21St Century Conservation includes restoring nature in the communities that we design and build.

CHAPTER 8

ECOREGIONS

Queen's Crown (*Rhodiola rhodantha*)

One of the extraordinary things about this region is the dramatic change in elevation from the prairie at 4,000 to 6,000 feet above sea level to peaks over 14,000 feet high. This results in the relatively close proximity of four distinct life zones, making this one of the most ecologically diverse regions in the US. In the Rocky Mountain region, one can travel quickly through several different life zones by changing elevation. A drive of just a few hours is comparable to traveling hundreds of miles north.

Because the states are political boundaries and not confined to specific "ecoregions," the term "native plants" is more accurately applied to zones that may span several states. Queen's crown (*Rhodiola rhodantha*) grows in Colorado's alpine zone, but that does not necessarily mean that it will grow elsewhere in the state without specific care. From the perspective of ecoregions, Denver has more in common with Cheyenne, Wyoming, and Las Vegas, New Mexico, than it does with Aspen or Vail, Colorado.

As the great plains rise toward the Rocky Mountains, the land becomes increasingly dry. Colorado's high plains receive an average of 12 to 14 inches of precipitation per year. This arid environment is dominated by grasses similar to other steppe environments globally, including Central Asia, South Africa, and high-altitude portions of Europe.

The high plains of Eastern Colorado are part of the shortgrass prairie ecosystem, which covers eastern Montana and southeastern Wyoming, southwestern South Dakota, western Nebraska, eastern Colorado, western Kansas, eastern New Mexico, western Oklahoma, and the Texas Panhandle.

The shortgrass prairie is distinguished from the mid- and tallgrass prairies to the east by the predominance of warm-season short grasses, including buffalo grass (*Buchloe dactyloides*), blue grama (*Bouteloua gracilis*), sideoats grama (*Bouteloua curtipendula*), and cool-season wheatgrasses that can thrive in prolonged periods of drought. Winter storms tend to hit the Rockies' western slopes and are driven higher, skipping over the Front Range to deliver their moisture further to the east. In addition, winter winds driven into the high atmosphere are compressed by the air pressure, causing them to become warmer. These Chinook winds can evaporate what little powdery snow hits the ground in winter before it can penetrate the soil. Often the most significant amounts of moisture arrive in spring when the warming waters in the Gulf of Mexico send moisture north, often arriving as snow dumped along the Front Range.

Many cities and towns along the Front Range, including Loveland and Fort Collins, border the prairie on their eastern edges and rise into the foothills on the west. Prairie soils are primarily alkaline clay. The soils change to less alkaline at the foothills zone (5,500 to 8,000 ft.

Due to extreme variation in elevation there are five distinct ecoregions, sometimes referred to as Life Zones within Colorado.

Pawnee National Grassland

above sea level), predominantly made up of decomposed granite. Foothills along the Front Range are part of the Dakota Formation created by the upward thrust of the Rocky Mountains around sixty-five million years ago. Conifers like ponderosa pine (*Pinus ponderosa*) and Rocky Mountain juniper (*Juniperus scopulorum*), which may appear on rocky outcroppings on the prairie, become more common in the foothills and montane zones.

The montane zone (8,000 to 10,000 feet above sea level), sometimes described as the ponderosa pine savanna, is where the fire cycle historically limited the number of trees and created a grassland studded with mature ponderosa pines. The mature ponderosa's pumpkin-orange bark and self-thinning of lower branches made them fire-resistant. Meadows filled with grasses and wildflowers receive moisture from afternoon thunderstorms in summer, frequently making them lusher than lower-elevation grasslands. Extensive groves of aspen (*Populous tremuloides*) trees cover much of the land where moisture is sufficient to support them. This zone contains the greatest diversity of plants and animals in the Rocky Mountain West.

Sometimes an upper montane zone is identified separately as the portions of the montane zone where lodgepole pine (*Pinus contorta*) and limber pine (*Pinus flexilis*) begin to emerge in a much-denser forest. Both the lodgepole pine and ponderosa pine have died in large numbers over the last few decades, increasing the fuel load for wildfires. This results from both stress on trees due to overcrowding and fire suppression, as well as a warming climate. Mountain pine beetle and ips beetle infections have also increased due to the crowding of trees and milder winters.

In the subalpine zone (10,000 to 11,500 feet above sea level), Engelmann spruce (*Picea engelmannii*) and subalpine fir (*Abies lasiocarpa*) predominate in a heavy forest canopy. There are few animal species in the subalpine zone, virtually limited to red squirrels and Clark's nutcrackers, the predominant animals in this zone. The subalpine forest is critical for storing snowpack that feeds municipal water supplies along the Front Range. At the upper edge of the subalpine zone is an area referred to as the *Krumholtz* ("twisted wood" in German), where the winds sculpt the trees into fantastic shapes and stunted "elfin forests."

Dakota Formation "hogbacks"

Montane meadow and upright blue beardtongue (*Penstemon virgatus A. Gray*)

The subalpine forest feeds municipal water supplies along Colorado's Front Range.

Above the tree line, the alpine zone (11,500 feet above sea level and above), like the arctic tundra, bursts into bloom in late spring and early summer in a brief but glorious season. Here elk migrate to graze on the alpine tundra in summer. A few animals living in the zone, including marmots and pikas, gain as much weight as possible in the short summer months to survive the long winter. Ptarmigans, birds also found in the arctic, survive the brutal alpine winter subsisting on conifer needles and alder twigs.

In addition, the riparian zone threads its way through the other zones wherever sufficient moisture is present. The riparian zone includes river and pond edges, wetlands, and playas, ephemeral wetlands that may be inundated in spring but appear as low-lying grasslands in the dryer season. According to Robert H. Wayland III of the U.S. Environmental Protection Agency, "Riparian areas comprise less than one percent of the land area of most western States, yet up to 80 percent of all wildlife species in this region of the country are dependent upon riparian areas for at least part of their life cycles."

Krumholtz means "twisted wood" in German.

The riparian zone is critical habitat for 80% of wildlife species in the West.

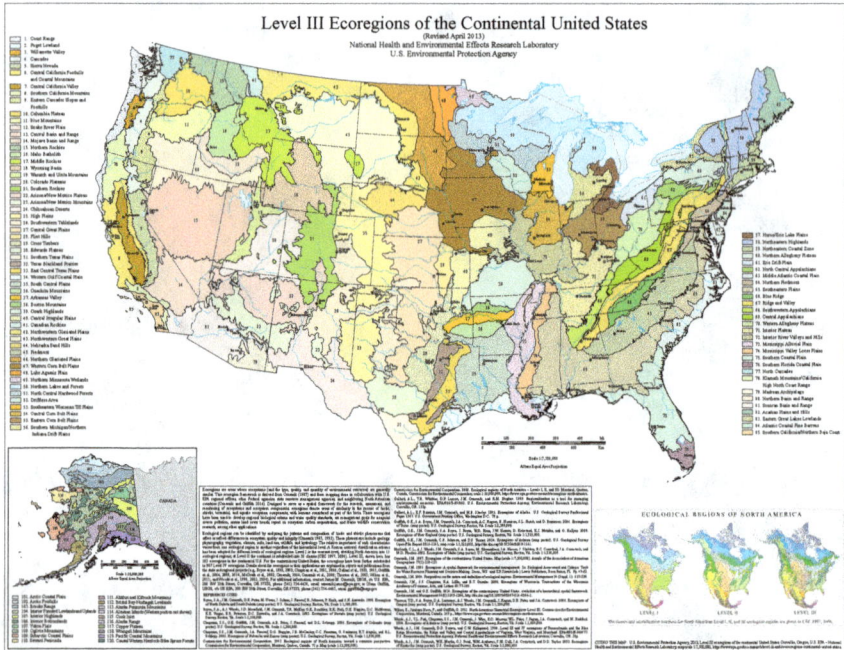

Omernick's Ecoregions map (For full size map see www.epa.gov)

Omernick's Ecoregions Map was created by the EPA. It uses climate, precipitation, soil type, vegetation, and other factors to define distinct ecoregions within the United States. State boundaries do not conform to ecoregions, and no ecoregion is confined to a specific state.

For the discussion of restoration, we will focus primarily on the lower elevation grasslands of the Rocky Mountain Region, where the majority of the human population lives. The shortgrass prairie is the area that has been most impacted by agriculture and land development and is considered to be the most degraded ecosystem in North America.

CHAPTER 9

HOW TO ESTABLISH AND MANAGE NATIVE GRASS

t's important to note that merely planting native grass does not make a prairie. A real prairie is like an old-growth forest that requires centuries, if not millennia, to establish. Once destroyed, it does not reestablish quickly. By far, the most valuable and rare natural areas are those that existed prior to agriculture and development, which have been carefully preserved.

Assessing a site before development and preserving existing vegetation requires foresight and sensitivity that is rare within the world of land development. Preserving existing vegetation on a building site requires tremendous discipline, and sometimes the threat of fines imposed on contractors to observe preservation and protect boundaries. It also requires long-term management oversight to prevent landscape contractors from coming into areas that have been carefully preserved and killing high-value native vegetation along with weeds.

Native vegetation, when undisturbed by excessive grazing, cultivation, or development, can typically fend off the incursion of invasive weed species. We call this homeostasis, the tendency toward a relatively stable equilibrium. When land is disturbed, it is susceptible to weed invasion. At that point, it will require some method of weed control, ideally followed by some type of revegetation plan. If weeds are not managed, and native vegetation is not reestablished, it will result in successive generations of weeds. Native grass, once established, will have minimal weed incursions if appropriately managed.

Over the past several years, there has been a growing interest in utilizing native grass in common areas in urban and suburban developments. In the Rocky Mountain West, this makes particularly good sense because of the increasing demands on our limited water resources and the corresponding rise in water cost. The question of why to restore native grasses is woven together with the issues of economics, aesthetics, community expectations, wildlife habitat, water, and quality of life.

One of the things that makes working with native grassland restoration challenging is that it doesn't fit into typical landscape construction timelines. Without irrigation, establishing native grass could take years. Even with irrigation, the prolonged "ugly duckling" phase of native open space can be challenging for developers and HOAs with many eyes and opinions surrounding the project. It is essential to establish realistic timelines and expectations and then communicate them to ensure that all parties involved understand the challenges and the unpredictability of this type of restoration.

If the newly seeded grass is irrigated, it should remain constantly moist. Depending on whether the irrigation heads are pop-ups that deliver water more quickly or rotors that make slow rotations and need to run longer, water cycles should be anywhere from ten to thirty minutes long, three times a day. An irrigation system is costly, but it can move the establishment forward by years. After the grass has established, however, irrigation will virtually never be needed again. Leaving PVC, metal, and plastic irrigation lines in the ground for all time is in many ways counter to the goals of environmental stewardship. If it is feasible, it is worth considering installing an above-ground system and removing it after year one.

Once the irrigation is activated, it is essential to limit incursions into the natural area. Seedlings have not yet developed strong enough root systems to anchor them firmly in the soil or to help them recover from damage. Moist soil also compacts more readily than dry soil. Areas rutted by vehicles and foot traffic will not establish well and will become weedy later.

Grasses are divided into warm-season and cool-season species. Warm-season short grasses, such as buffalo grass (*Buchloe dactyloides*), blue grama (*Bouteloua gracilis*), and sideoats grama (*Bouteloua curtipendula*), are common on the high plains (also called the shortgrass prairie) because they thrive in hot and dry conditions. Warm-season grasses do not emerge from dormancy until late spring. They flower and produce seeds in late summer and early fall.

Warm-season tall grasses include yellow Indiangrass (*Sorghastrum nutans*), big bluestem grass (*Andropogon gerardii*), and switchgrass (*Panicum virgatum*). These grasses are predominant on the eastern portions of the great plains, where the annual precipitation of 30–35 inches per year is double that of the shortgrass prairie. However, tall grasses do grow in the low-lying portions of the high plains where sufficient moisture exists. These grasses do particularly well in stormwater ponds and conveyances that are periodically inundated but not saturated year-round. Warm-season tall grasses are particularly beautiful when their seed heads form and the plants turn to gold, orange, and red in autumn.

Buffalo grass (*Buchloe dactyloides*)

Sideoats grama (*Bouteloua curtipendula*)

Blue grama (*Bouteloua gracilis*)

Yellow Indian grass (*Sorghastrum nutans*)

Big bluestem grass (*Andropogon gerardii*)

Switch grass (*Panicum virgatum*)

Warm-season tall grasses

Cool season grasses, Western wheatgrass (*Agropyron smithii*)

Many cool-season grasses are common on the shortgrass prairie as well, particularly various wheatgrasses, Junegrass (*Koeleria macrantha*), and Canada wildrye (*Elymus canadensis*). Cool-season grasses emerge from dormancy in early spring. They flower and produce seeds in the late spring and early summer (May and June). Because these grasses begin to establish earlier in the season, they can predominate by outcompeting other plants when conditions are favorable.

Generally, it's a good idea to include both cool and warm-season grasses in a seed mix to create more diversity, to extend the peak growing season, and ensure the successful establishment of the seed.

Seed mixes may perform differently when planted at different times of the year. Winter or early spring seeding may favor the establishment of cool-season grasses. If cool-season grasses germinate first, they may use up the available moisture and outcompete the warm season grasses.

Mowing at specific times during the season can help to shift the balance toward the warm-season grasses. Cool-season grasses typically complete their growth for the year by late May. We have often observed that a late spring mowing suppresses cool-season species by interrupting seed production and allowing warm-season species to emerge.

In a prairie environment, grassland succession is dependent on fire or grazing. These occurrences, particularly fire, help to remove old vegetative cover and initiate a cycle of regeneration. Periodic mowing can, to some extent, replicate these influences, but excessive mowing undermines the health of native grass and ultimately produces more incursion of weeds by exposing soil to sunlight and allowing the weed seed bank to germinate. Mowing also stresses the grass, causing it to decline.

Most lawn-mowing companies mow turfgrass (Kentucky bluegrass and tall fescue) too short. The ideal mowing height for turf grass is 3.5 to 4 inches. When grass is scalped, it becomes stressed, and the soil has more exposure to sunlight resulting in more weed germination and more evaporation. High plains grasses are adapted to tolerate a limited amount of mowing (historically in the form of grazing by bison and other prairie animals), but excessive mowing will deplete their energy reserves. This impairs their ability to grow and withstand damage. Unless the grass is being over-seeded to change the species' make up or to regenerate an area, native grass should never be mowed shorter than 5 inches tall.

We have often gone to look at failing native grass areas in HOAs and other developed sites and found large expanses of bindweed where the grass has been excessively mowed. Bindweed thrives on mowing and grazing because they reduce shade and competition. The simple equation is that mowing equals weeds.

We have many good examples of mown and unmown grass of the same species makeup, side by side, and the difference in the number of weeds is immediately evident. Unmown native grass can exist for years with no mowing at all. The old grass growth helps to shade out weeds, creating its own mulch, while the newly emerging grass can easily grow through it.

CHAPTER 10

WEEDS, WEED, WEEDS!

B ecause the shortgrass prairie has been heavily disturbed, and our dry climate makes restoration a slow process, our region has tremendous problems with weeds. Many residential developments are built on land that was previously farmed. The native vegetation has been destroyed, and invasive plant species abound. It doesn't help when adjacent properties have unmanaged weeds as they produce seeds that will end up in the seed bank. It's important to keep undeveloped lots in cover crops or seed with native grass until development comes in. Never introduce potentially invasive, non-native grasses that will be hard to eradicate later.

Any time the ground is disturbed, the seed bank will become activated and begin to grow. The seed bank may contain valuable native plants, as well as weeds. Many of the weeds that show up will be annuals, which live one year, set seeds, and die. If not allowed to go to seed, annual weeds will be significantly diminished in the second year. For this reason, a newly seeded stand of native grass will be unsightly in the first year.

Flowering plants are divided into monocots (plants that germinate sending up one seedling leaf or "cotyledon") and dicots (plants that germinate sending up two cotyledons). Herbicides are sometimes categorized by their ability to kill dicots only (broadleaf plants) or both dicots and monocots. That's how herbicides can be applied directly to grasses (monocots) without killing them but will kill broadleaf weeds.

Herbicides typically cannot be used in year one of native grass establishment because, even if they are not intended for monocots, they can burn tiny grass seedlings.

Mowing is the primary weed control strategy in year one. It can be a real challenge to hold back on mowing until the timing is right, just before the weeds are about to set seeds. If the weeds are mowed too early, many will recover and flower again on much shorter stems. Picture dandelions that flower two inches tall after the mower has gone over them. Mowing plants just before they set seed weakens weedy plants, but most will recover and try again to produce seeds. Typically, a stand of native grass will be mowed four or five times throughout the first season. Mowing will not harm the germinating native grass, which will only grow a few inches tall in the first year.

It can be beneficial to include a cover crop in the grass seed mix. A cover crop can help to reduce the number of weeds through competition. A cover crop can be particularly beneficial when there is a need to establish vegetative cover for erosion control, which is a requirement in some municipalities. It will also look a lot better to the uneducated observer for whom "grass is grass." A good cover crop will germinate quickly but will not outcompete native grasses once they are established.

On a restoration project in a natural area, an ecologist would most likely insist on a sterile cover crop. Within HOA open space, we have often used annual rye (*Lolium multiflorum*), which is quick to germinate and dies out after a few seasons. We have also noticed that annual rye seems to fill the exact ecological niche of cheatgrass (*Bromus tectorum*), a persistent annual invasive grass. Cheatgrass typically germinates in the fall and remains semi-green throughout the winter. Because of its early start, it often outcompetes other grasses because whoever gets there first wins.

Perennial weeds can typically be treated with herbicide at the end of season one. Plants can also be hand-pulled if the manpower is available. Some plants, however, such as Canada thistle (*Cirsium arvense*), will persist due to their extensive root system. Hand pulling Canada thistle does not help due to its extensive root system, and pulling can stimulate more thistle shoot and root growth. Mowing can weaken the plants and limit seed production but will not eradicate thistles. An herbicide called aminopyralid is used on thistle. It is spot sprayed on thistle at an extremely low dilution rate, and the EPA approves it for application up to the water's edge in wetlands where thistles typically grow. Though it persists for a long time in the soil, making it effective for weed control, it has extremely low toxicity to humans and other animals.

In year two of native grass establishment, annual weeds should be greatly reduced. Where annuals weeds appear, they can be spot-sprayed or mowed. Often the weedy spots will be areas where the grass did not germinate well, and reseeding may be necessary for these spots. The management of native grass is extremely important and can determine the long-term success or failure of a restoration project. Once established, native grass requires no fertilizing and little or no watering. Both would most likely increase the incursion of weeds.

In high traffic areas, such as HOAs and business parks, it's common practice to mow a strip alongside walkways. These "beauty bands," as they're often called, provide a bit of definition between the open space and the walkway. They keep grasses from hanging over the trail and help to alleviate anxieties about snakes or other wildlife adjacent to the trail. We typically mow every two to four weeks starting in early to mid-April and stop mowing in mid-June to allow warm-season grasses, which are often more delicate, to go to seed.

Pre-existing, invasive, cool-season grasses

Invasive cool-season grasses are introduced species that were originally planted for animal forage or erosion stabilization. Though they have their uses, they are hard to eradicate once established. Planting native grass over invasive grasses will yield little more than a frustrating and costly mistake.

Common grasses in the invasive cool-season group include smooth brome (*Bromus inermis*), crested wheatgrass (*Argropyron cristata*), orchardgrass (*Dactylis glomerata*), quack grass (*Elymus repens*), and timothy (*Phleum pratense*). Before planting, it is necessary to eradicate

Warm season grasses display their beautiful seeds in fall when edges are left unmown.

these cool-season grasses. This can best be accomplished by spraying an herbicide in the fall when plants are actively growing, then spraying the regrowth again in the spring. This is usually enough to knock down the cool-season grasses. However, a seed bank may still exist. Tilling in a succession of cover crops over a period of years could also be an effective, albeit slow process, for eradicating invasive grasses.

It is possible to seed warm-season grasses and continue to spot spray invasive cool-season grasses that may reinfiltrate if the spraying is done when warm-season grasses are dormant. We have used this technique in wetlands where reed canary grass (*Phalaris arundinacea*) outcompetes native wetland plants. When appropriately timed, this can knock down invasive grasses and release native wetland plants from competition.

Why Invasive Species Matter

Some readers may be asking at this point why an environmental organization is advocating the use of herbicides. HPEC is a science-based organization focused on ecological restoration. Our staff members

invasive cool-season grasses, smooth brome (*Bromus inermis*)

have degrees in range ecology, agronomy, restoration ecology, and horticulture. We know of no organization that is effectively restoring habitat on a large scale without using herbicides as at least one of their management tools.

The condition of the shortgrass prairie along Colorado's Front Range can be compared to a hospital patient. Chemotherapy and radiation are not recommended as a lifestyle for anyone, but they have saved or extended the lives of countless critically ill patients. The goal of restoring native vegetation is to restore equilibrium and allow areas to thrive under natural processes with minimal human intervention. For long-range management of native vegetation, very low amounts of herbicide are used on species-specific targets. The current model of conventional landscaping is, by comparison, highly dependent on irrigation, herbicide, fertilizer, and machinery that produces 5 percent of the US greenhouse gas emissions.

The cultivation of the prairie and the introduction of invasive plant species from arid high-altitude zones in Europe and Asia present significant challenges to restoration. Once in their new range, invasive plant species typically do not have the natural insect predators that helped keep them in check in their native range. Operating outside of these native plant/insect agreements, negotiated within the subtle balance of coevolving species, invasive species expand rampantly, often out-competing natives. The destruction of wild plants and competition with weeds reduces forage for native insects.

Throughout the world, plants have developed chemical means of repelling insects. Often, specific insects have coevolved with the plants, developing a tolerance for these specific chemicals. These insects are frequently the same species that pollinate the plants. The vast number of these intricate plant/pollinator relationships is not fully known.

An example of the symbiotic relationship between native plants and insects can be found in the relationship between the yucca plant (*Yucca glauca*) and the yucca moth (*Tegeticula yuccasella*.) The yucca plant can only be pollinated by the yucca moth. The moth, in turn, lays its eggs in the developing flower before it develops into fruit. The female moth leaves a pheromone scent that lets other yucca moths know that eggs have already been laid on this plant. When the larvae hatch, they eat some (but not all) of the yucca seeds as they're developing, and both species survive for another generation in the process.

Plants turn the sun's energy into leaves, which insects eat. Insects provide a critical source of protein for birds. According to Douglass Tallamy, in the book *Bringing Nature Home*, insects provide 96 percent of all terrestrial birds' diet, particularly during the breeding season.

For this reason, restoring native plant populations is essential to restoring habitat.

Weeds do provide some benefits however. They often establish quickly, helping to reduce soil erosion. Many weeds are species that have been carried around the world for human purposes, including medicinal and ornamental value. Others were carried along in crop seed. Russian thistle (*Salsola tragus*), the iconic tumbleweed of Western movies, is a Russian native said to have traveled to South Dakota in bags of flaxseed. For specific herbicide recommendations, consult your County Agricultural Extension Service.

We have noticed that in any given year, we see a predominance of a particular type of weeds. These predominant weed species changes year to year based on subtle changes in temperature and rainfall and

Monarch butterflies require milkweed plants during their larval stage.

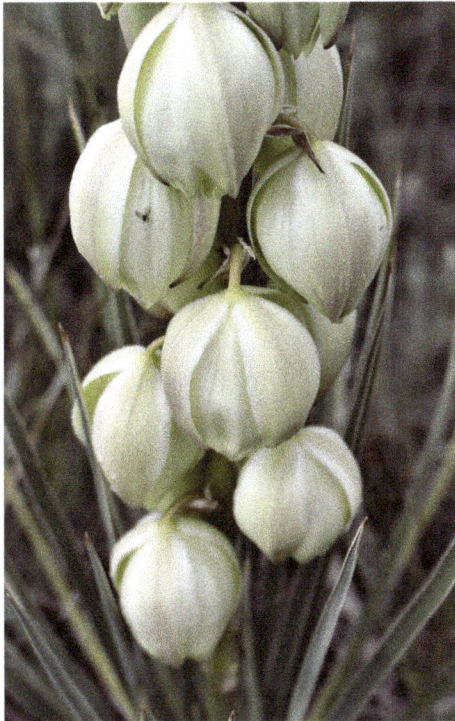

Great Plains yucca (*Yucca glauca*)

White primrose (*Oenothera albicaulis*) and Rocky Mountain bee plant (*Cleome serrulata*)

the timing of weather events, which can favor the germination of specific species. Not only will we have a particular weed outbreak on the properties that we manage, but we notice all other natural areas in our region having the same weed occurrence.

In September of 2013, we had a foot of rain in one day that caused massive flooding in Northern Colorado. The following spring, we and everyone else saw an explosion of cheatgrass like we had never seen before. That same year, the nearby Pawnee National Grassland had a super bloom of native Oenothera albicaulis (white-stemmed evening primrose) that looked like snow covering the ground as far as the eye could see.

CHAPTER 11

SEEDING NATIVE GRASS

O nce a plan for the open space has been created and seed mixes specified, a contractor is chosen to implement the project. It is extremely helpful to have a project manager familiar with the subtleties of the design to oversee the installation and ensure that things are done correctly. Prior to seeding, verify that the seeding contractor has cleaned out seed boxes to remove any residual seed from previous seeding jobs. Inspect seed tags onsite to verify that all species are correct before any seeding is done. The following section is the seeding specification that we use within Centerra and elsewhere.

Soil Preparation

Fertilizer. Phosphorus is typically deficient in Colorado soils. Because phosphorus is a promoter of root growth, it is extremely beneficial to new seedlings. Phosphorus is also immobile in clay soils, so it needs to be applied before tillage work to be incorporated into the root zone. Additional nitrogen typically results in an influx of weeds. It's best to have your soil tested, making sure that the testing laboratory knows that recommendations are for native grass. Often no soil amendment is needed.

Tillage. Tillage is one of the most important steps that is often over-looked. All areas shall be thoroughly tilled to a depth of 6–8 inches after the soil amendments have been applied. This can be accomplished with rototilling machinery or, in larger areas, agricultural machinery such as chisel plows and/or discs.

Fine Grading. After tillage is complete, all areas shall be fine graded with a soil finisher. Grading for turf areas will require more detail than native areas. Turf areas shall be smooth, even, and one inch below adjacent sidewalks and curbs. The grade for native areas can be left somewhat rougher or less detailed because these areas will be managed with a larger class of machinery, i.e., tractors and brush hog-type rotary mowers.

Native Short Grass Mix

(Can be left unmown adjacent to formal landscaped areas)

Seeded at 2 lbs. PLS/1000 sq ft or 86 lbs./acre.

Buffalo grass *(Buchloe dactyloides)*, "Cody" or 'Bowie" 40 percent

Blue grama *(Bouteloua gracilis)*, "Alma" or "Bad River" 20 percent

Sideoats grama (*Bouteloua curtipendula*), "Vaughn" or "El Reno" 20 percent

Slender wheatgrass (*Elymus trachycaulus)* 20 percent

Native seeding must be completed with a native grass drill with three-seed boxes capable of metering and applying fine seed, fluffy seed, and smooth seed. These three types of seed are designated on the seed mix labels. Examples are smooth seed—wheatgrasses, fluffy seed—yellow Indian grass, and fine seed—alkali sacaton. For the turf grasses or other mixes, small areas can be hand broadcast, or a Brillion drill or other appropriate drill should be used.

Native seed mixes must be ordered so that fluffy seed, fine seed, and smooth seed are bagged separately and can be placed in the appropriate seed box for application. Tags for all mixes, including the native seed, must be provided for inspection prior to any seed being planted.

Upland Native Areas for Open Space Areas

Lbs. PLS/acre seed box designation

Slender wheatgrass. (*Elymus trachycaulus*) 3 lbs. Smooth

Western wheatgrass. (*Pascopyrum smithii*) "Rosana" 3 lbs. Smooth

Green needlegrass. (*Nassella viridula*) "Lodorm" 1 lb. Smooth

Canada wildrye. (*Elymus canadensis*) "Mandan" 1 lb. Smooth

Beardless wildrye. (*Leymus triticoides*) "Shoshone" 0.5 lb. Smooth

Blue grama. (*Bouteloua gracilis*) "Bad River" 0.5 lb. Fluffy

Sideoats grama. (*Bouteloua curtipendula*) "Vaughn" 1.5 lbs. Fluffy

Little bluestem. (*Schizachyrium scoparium*) "Camper" 1.5 lbs. Fluffy

Yellow Indiangrass. (*Sorghastrum nutans*) "Tomahawk" or "Neb 54" 1 lb. Fluffy

Big bluestem. (*Andropogon gerardii*) "Pawnee" 1 lb. Fluffy

Switchgrass. (*Panicum virgatum*) 'Blackwell' 0.5 lb. Fine

Alkali sacaton. (*Sporobolus airoides*) 0.25 lb. Fine

Annual rye. 2 lbs. Smooth

Total 16.75 pounds pure live seed per acre

Erosion Control or Overlot Areas—for temporary soil stabilization
These areas are drill seeded with the following mix:

Slender wheatgrass. (*Elymus trachycaulus*) 5 Lbs.

Western wheatgrass. (*Pascopyrum smithii*) "Rosana" 3 lbs.

Canada wildrye. (*Elymus canadensis*) "Mandan" 3 lbs.

Total 11 pounds pure live seed per acre

If required, a cover crop like annual rye can be added to this mix.

Canada wildrye (*Elymus canadensis*)

Hydromulch. Native seed areas and turfgrass areas shall be mulched with virgin wood fiber hydromulch with steam-separable fibers. The rate of application shall be 2,500 lbs./acre. Straw mulch overlot areas or temporary erosion control seeding shall be mulched with weed-free certified straw at a rate of two tons/acre, crimped 3–4 inches into the soil surface. Hydromulch overspray must be cleaned off all sidewalks, fences, light poles, switch cabinets, and landscape material. When straw mulching is complete, all twine or bale wrap material must be picked up and removed.

A note about cultivars

According to the US Forest Service: "Grass cultivars are a distinct subset of a species, often intentionally bred to behave uniformly and predictably when grown in an environment to which the species is adapted. A cultivar (a portmanteau of 'cultivated variety'), also called a variety or a release, is given a unique trade name chosen by the breeder." Cultivar names are written in single quotation marks.

Plants will sometimes adapt into genotypes specific to local conditions. For this reason, many ecologists, when doing restoration work, will not use seed or cuttings collected from plants in differing altitudes or ecoregions.

In the ornamental nursery trade, a plant breeder may notice a plant with particularly showy characteristics. They may give that plant a special name and propagate it since these characteristics are not reliably replicated from seed produced by the plants if they are propagated vegetatively. This means that cuttings or cloning of the original plant are used in order to preserve ornamental characteristics.

One example of this is the immensely popular "Blond ambition" blue grama grass. It is blue grama (*Bouteloua gracilis*) that grows taller and larger, produces more seed heads, and has a distinctive golden color. It's a stunning plant. The potential downside of cultivars is that they represent one individual plant's genetics and reduce the genetic diversity of a population.

The genetic diversity of wild species is essential. Because blue grama (*Bouteloua gracilis*) grows from Texas to the Canadian prairie provinces, it is adaptable to a wide range of climate variations. Local variations in the plant may occur. Some would argue that introducing subtle differences in the timing of bloom or other variations could alter genetic traits of local plant populations. This could change characteristics with which local insects have coevolved.

An example would be insects that come out of dormancy when specific plants begin to bloom only to find them not in bloom or past blooming. This is a complex discussion, and ecologists, as well as horticulturists, take many different positions. At HPEC, we advocate for the use of native plants in general, and if those can be the local genetic ecotype, so much the better, but we don't see pollinators boycotting cultivars.

'Blond Ambition', a cultivar of blue grama grass (*Bouteloua gracilis*)

Rocky Mountain beardtongue (*Penstemon strictus*) and Nevada bumblebee

CHAPTER 12

WILDFLOWERS, SHRUBS, AND TREES IN NATIVE OPEN SPACE

Wildflowers

Aside from their aesthetic value, wildflowers help to increase plant species diversity in open space. Some products sold in garden centers would suggest that you can create a beautiful wildflower meadow by simply scattering seeds around. The fact is, creating a meadow with wildflowers is one of the most challenging things to achieve in horticulture, especially in Colorado.

One of the problems that comes with planting wildflowers on a large scale is that they are broadleaf plants, like many weeds, and cannot be treated with herbicide without damaging desirable species. For this reason, it's necessary to hand-pull weeds growing among wildflowers. This requires a maintenance team that can distinguish between wildflowers and weeds at all stages of development. It works well to create smaller islands of wildflowers that can be intensively managed during establishment and allowed to spread out into adjacent native grass over time.

Wildflowers often thrive in low-nutrient soil and do not compete well with grasses. Choose spots where your native grass is not coming in well for wildflower islands. It can also be helpful to add a gritty,

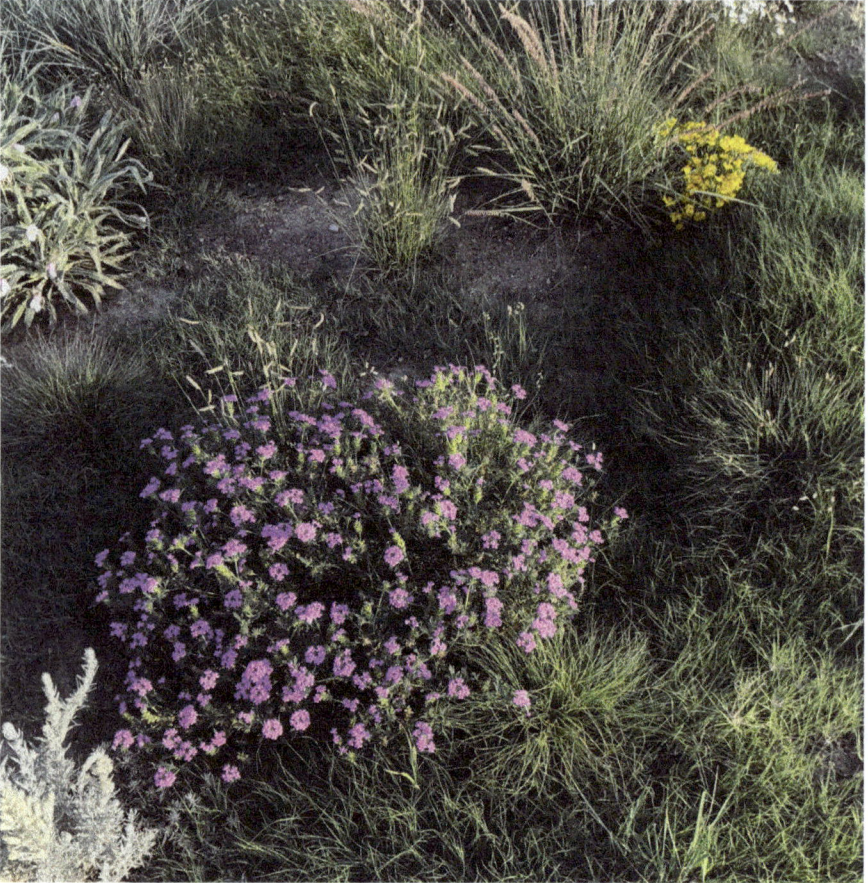

Prairie Wildflowers: Tufted evening primrose (*Oenothera caespitosa*), plains verbena (*verbena bipinnatifida*) blackfoot daisy (*Melampodium leucanthum*)

well-drained material that includes sand and gravel. We have created tall berms of road base mixed with native soil and seeded wildflowers directly in them with excellent results.

Seeds can be scattered on the surface of the soil and raked in lightly. It helps to scatter the seeds in fall or winter just before a snowstorm. The snow prevents birds from finding and eating the seeds, and it helps the seeds to get pressed down into the soil without burying them too deeply.

When choosing appropriate wildflower species, take your soil type, elevation, and available soil moisture into consideration. It helps to visit nearby natural areas to observe what may be growing. In our area,

Seeding wildflowers in "islands" of gravelly soil. Wildflower seeding rates vary from 4–10 lbs. per acre depending on the species. (Photo credit: Jack Van Vleet)

fringed sage (*Artemisia frigida*), scarlet globemallow (*Sphaeralcea coccinea*), and hairy golden aster (*Heterotheca villosa*) are common natives that thrive on our prairie clay. Some natives such as Lewis blue flax (*Linum lewisii)*, blanketflower (*Gaillardia aristata*), and Bigelow's tansyaster (*Machaeranthera bigelovii)* are popular for restoration because they establish quickly and spread aggressively. Beware of seed mixes commonly sold at garden centers, which contain non-native seeds such as bachelor buttons (*Centaurea cyanus*, also called cornflower) and babies' breath (*Gypsophila, spp.)*.

Wildflower seed is extremely expensive. At HPEC, we collect bags of seed from our native plant demonstration gardens and save them for restoration projects and propagation in our nursery. If you collect wild seed, always make sure to have the landowner's permission and avoid over-collecting seed and depleting the native population.

To collect seed, identify the species of interest in the landscape and notice when the flowers turn into seed heads, from late spring to fall, depending on the species. Track them as they dry out and turn brown so that you don't miss your collection window for viable seeds. Break

Wildflowers at Old Canal Park: Blanket flower (*Gaillardia aristata*), Prince's plume (*Stanleya pinnata*), Lewis Flax (*Linum lewisii*), Desert four o'clock (*Mirabilis multiflora*), Rocky Mountain bee plant (*Cleome serrulata*).

or cut off the seed heads and place them in a paper bag so they can dry out. Storing seed heads in plastic bags should be avoided as they can cause them to become moldy.

Once the seed heads are thoroughly dry, seeds of some species will literally fall out, while others will need to be cleaned to remove all plant debris. This is done in various ways, including using sieves of various sizes. After they're cleaned of debris, the seeds are stored in a cool, dry place. It's helpful to track the date and location the seeds were collected for future reference. Desiccant packets found in foods like beef jerky can be placed with the seeds to help keep them dry until needed.

When growing plants in a greenhouse, many native seeds require "cold, moist stratification," where the seeds are placed in a plastic bag with damp sand and placed in a refrigerator for thirty to ninety days, depending on the species. This process replicates winter conditions and allows the seed coating to break and the seedlings to sprout.

This is when it's essential that all plant debris be removed to minimize mold growth that can kill the seedlings. Some seeds, such as

Dried seed head

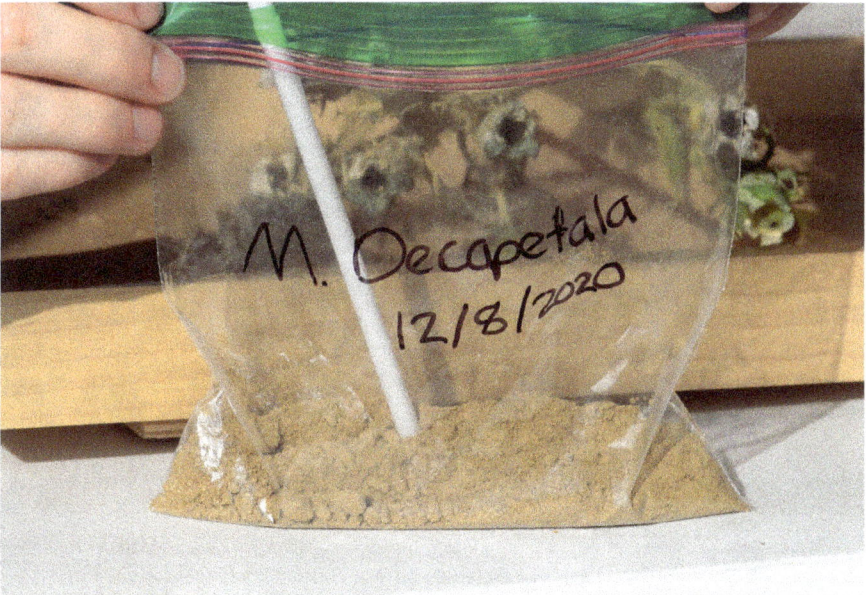

Seed bag ready for cold stratification

Golden banner (*Thermopsis divaricarpa*), have a hard coating that needs to be cracked for them to germinate. In a natural setting, this occurs through exposure to freeze-thaw cycles or by passing through an animal's digestive tract. For collected seeds, this "scarification" can be done by scratching each seed with sandpaper.

After the cold stratification period, seed can be sown in trays and transplanted to individual pots when their second set of true leaves develop. A simpler way to do this is to sow seed directly in pots and place them outdoors, where they will go through the cold stratification process naturally. Sow seeds in pots, label them, and cover with a thin layer of small gravel to hold seeds in place. Seeds will germinate in spring when the seasonal conditions are right.

Native shrubs and trees provide valuable cover, berries, insects, nest sites, and other resources for migratory, nesting, and wintering birds. Organizing shrubs correctly replicates natural habitat, and placing them in the right locations will eliminate the need to water them once they become established.

Hydrological Zones. American plum (*Prunus americana*) grows in the drainage in the foreground. On the dryer slopes behind are rabbitbrush (*Ericameria nauseosa*) and three-leaf sumac (*Rhus trilobata*). Rocky Mountain juniper (*Juniperus scopulorum*) and ponderosa pine (*Pinus ponderosa*) populate the dryest rocky outcroppings.

In the Rocky Mountain West, the flowering of shrubs in spring and the colors of their autumn foliage reveal patterns that may be imperceptible at other times of the year. These patterns in the landscape provide subtle clues to the ways that plants are arranged in nature based on available moisture. People familiar with these patterns can tell a lot about the hydrology of a natural setting by how plants are organized.

Where cottonwood trees are found, there is very often an understory of riparian shrubs, including chokecherries (*Prunus virginiana var. melanocarpa*), golden currant (*Ribes aureum*), snowberry (*Symphoricarpos occidentalis*), and Woods' rose (*Rosa woodsii*).

When landscapers use these plants, they often space them far apart in small groupings, but when they grow in the wild, they create multi-tiered thickets growing literally on top of each other. There may be several reasons for this. Birds perch in cottonwood trees, and their droppings contain the seeds of the berries they eat, increasing the chances for the shrubs to get started below the trees. Cottonwood trees offer protection from sun and wind, which helps shrubs to get established.

Chokecherry (*Prunus virginiana var. melanocarpa*)

Golden currant (*Ribes aureum*)

Western snowberry (*Symphoricarpos occidentalis*)

Woods' rose (*Rosa woodsii*)

Although cottonwood trees consume a lot of water, they collaborate rather than compete with the shrubs. Large cottonwoods help to pull moisture into the shrubs' root zones. The cottonwoods hydraulically redistributing water from lower portions of the soil profile may help shrubs survive during dry periods. This multitiered arrangement of woody plants also provides an ideal habitat for birds, insects, small mammals, reptiles, and amphibians.

American plum (*Prunus americana*) often grows in extensive colonies, on moist slopes, away from other shrubs. Wild plums have a distinct characteristic of blooming in early spring before leaves emerge. The intensely fragrant white blossoms are highly attractive to bees. Research indicates that pollinators may have helped select for early bloom in this species, especially when they are in full sun because the pollinators that come out early in the year need to be sun-warmed to provide pollination services.

Redtwig dogwood *(Cornus sericea)* grows at the water's edge and can tolerate short periods of inundation or drought. Coyote willow (*Salix exigua*) creates a solid screen providing shelter for birds and

American plum (*Prunus americana*)

other wildlife. It should not be planted with other plants, which it will likely out-compete, or where its uncontrolled spread may be considered a problem.

Shrubby cinquefoil (*Potentilla fruticosa*) is a plant native to wet meadows in the montane zone. False indigo bush (*Amorpha fruticosa*) can be included along with other riparian prairie shrubs. Its cousin leadplant (*Amorpha canescens*) requires a slightly drier zone. On drier uplands in foothills and prairie zones, mountain mahogany (*Cercocarpus montanus*), three-leaf sumac (*Rhus trilobata*), and rubber rabbitbrush (*Ericameria nauseosa*) can be found. Saltbush (*Atriplex canescens*) is particularly suited to alkaline prairie clay.

All of these plants give us clues about the moisture content and soil type of a site. When we know where plants want to be, we can design landscapes that require little or no water because they are in the correct place to support them.

Too often, landscape designers attempt to apply a streetscape aesthetic when incorporating woody plants into native open space. Woody plants in nature do not grow as evenly spaced trees or modest groupings

Redtwig dogwood (*Cornus sericea*)

False indigo bush (*Amorpha fruticosa*)

Mountain mahogany (*Cercocarpus montanus*)

Three-leaf sumac (*Rhus trilobata*)

Rubber rabbit brush (*Ericameria nauseosa*)

The fall blooming rubber rabbitbrush (*Ericameria nauseosa*) is frequently visited by the American painted lady butterfly (*Vanessa virginiensis*).

of shrubs; they grow in multitiered thickets. The arrangement of these thickets has particular benefit for wildlife, providing both forage and cover. This bedded effect also helps to minimize tedious and costly mowing around small groups of shrubs and individual trees, so grouping them together also makes management easier.

When woody plants are grouped in thickets, cottonwoods are typically in the center with an understory of taller chokecherries and golden currants. Woods' rose or snowberry are placed in a lower tier on the outer edge of the thicket. It's a logical arrangement that looks beautiful when the plants are established.

This type of grouping is also a good strategy for ensuring the successful establishment of these plants. Young shrub transplants do not compete very well with grasses. When shrub beds are mulched with a four to six-inch layer of coarse wood chips (not mulch), it helps to hold in moisture and keep grasses out until shrubs are established. Mulch is typically made from shredded tree bark. Wood chips are made from whole tree branches and contain wood. Wood chips will not compact the way that mulch does. Beneficial mycorrhizae seem to thrive in wood chips and grow more rapidly than in mulch. The term mycorrhiza refers to a fungus that has a symbiotic relationship with the root systems of some plants. Mycorrhizae can aid plants in the uptake of water and nutrients from the soil and help plants to ward off pathogens.

In establishing a natural open space, we intend to introduce species that will reproduce and establish themselves. Like the concept of wildflower islands, shrubs within the thickets will begin to spring up in spots where the site can support them.

Trees provide many benefits in urban and suburban environments. They reduce the "urban heat island effect" that results from having reflective surfaces such as pavement and buildings. Trees provide beauty and cooling shade to city streets and create a more natural and aesthetically pleasing environment, sequester carbon, and provide habitat for birds and other wildlife. These environments, however, are not beneficial for the trees themselves. A tree on a city street often has an opening in the pavement of less than 100 square feet. The heat reflected from sidewalks can stress trees, making them susceptible to disease and pests and dramatically reducing their lifespan.

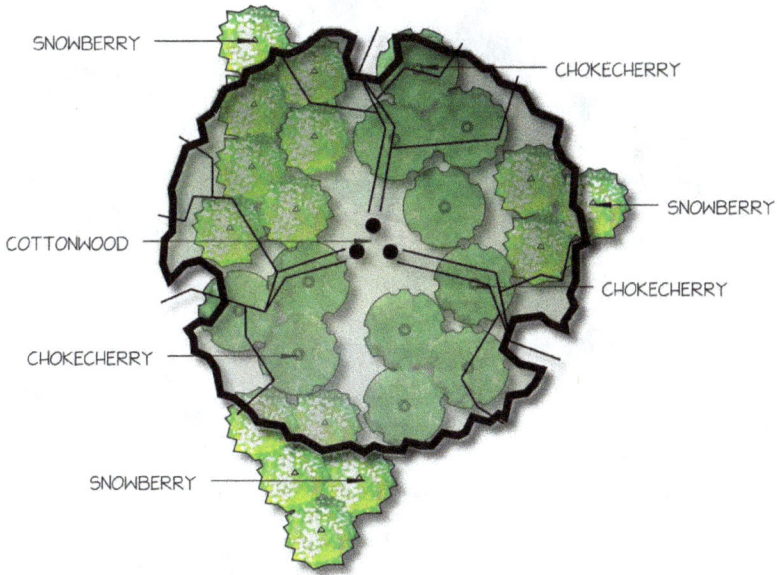

Woody plants arrangement (Drawing by J.R. Oldham)

In addition, the typical two to three-inch caliper tree loses up to 98 percent of its root system in the process of transplanting. In general, the smaller the tree, the better it transplants, and the quicker it grows. A three-quarter-inch caliper tree will often outpace larger transplants. By requiring two to three-inch caliper trees in landscape projects, many municipalities unintentionally undermine the success of trees.

Large stormwater drainage areas can provide an ideal environment for trees to grow in communities, providing the area is not inundated with water for long periods. Many trees grow in large, extended groves in the wild, often fusing their root systems for mutual nourishment and support. As water resources become an increasing concern for western cities, designing cities around constructed watersheds that support an urban forest that also sequesters carbon makes a great deal of sense.

This concept replicates something that existed in former times. Driving across the prairie, people may wonder how Native American tribes lived way out on these harsh and sunbaked plains. The fact is, they didn't: they may have crossed the plains or hunted there, but they

Wild thicket

Planted thicket

Cottonwood grove

lived and traveled along waterways. Rivers and creeks on the prairie can be identified from a great distance away as a strip of dark cotton-wood trees that blaze into gold in the fall. Within these cottonwood galleries, the air is cool and pleasant, the trees softly whisper, and birds sing in the branches of sheltering shrubs.

CHAPTER 13

ADAPTIVE MANAGEMENT

n 2007–2008, McWhinney, HPEC, Ark Ecological Services, and BHA Landscape Design created a document called the Centerra Stormwater Pond and Natural Areas Design Guidelines. The guidelines, which provide pond specifications that replicate natural wetlands, won a Land Stewardship Award from the American Society of Landscape Architects in 2009.

Under these guidelines, stormwater ponds and conveyances in Centerra are designed to replicate the wetlands' natural contours and structure. They have native plants arranged in communities according to available soil moisture, undulating edges vs. linear edges, and uneven pond bottoms vs. flat bottoms. The following is a distillation of that document.

Goals for habitat restoration include a focus on the protection or increase of plant and animal diversity, particularly rare or desirable species. A good restoration plan can also improve aesthetic appeal and create a beautiful landscape, with shade and resting spots that visitors can enjoy and appreciate without sacrificing the area's value for wildlife and plant habitat. The presence of water and screening vegetation can help shape visitor-use patterns and limit incursion into high-value habitat areas.

The way that natural areas are designed and managed also shapes their use and value to wildlife. Many HOA's that have ponds surrounded by turfgrass mowed right to the water's edge complain about the mess that Canada geese make, but it's the design and management practices that favor geese that are at fault. Mowing native areas between March 15th and June 15th can have devastating impact on ground-nesting birds such as meadowlarks and killdeer.

At HPEC, we manage the land with specific habitat goals in mind. As previously noted, wetland environments comprise less than 2 percent of Colorado's total land area and are utilized by 75 percent of all wildlife species at some point in their life cycle. Our goals focus on protecting and improving habitat for a variety of species, including grebes and ducks that breed here or stopover during the migration. We have also worked to improve fish habitat by sinking bundles of trees to provide cover for fish fingerlings. We have seen white pelicans fishing around these "brush reefs," which lets us know they are working.

An open space is not like a building that is built and then finished. It is driven by a dynamic process called adaptive management, in which the area is continually reassessed and refined. The process of design,

Killdeer eggs

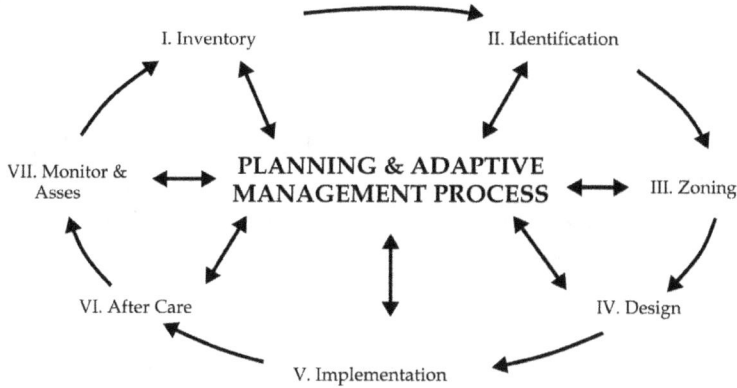

Adaptive Management illustration (Courtesy of BHA Design)

implementation, and management of habitat restoration areas is ongoing throughout the life of an open space and includes the following steps:

Inventory. Assess the ecological and cultural site conditions of the proposed natural area, detention pond, stream channel ("project area"), and the adjacent lands. Obtain information on the following: topography, slope, aspect, and hydrology of the site. Inventory existing native vegetation as well as weeds on the site.

Evaluate existing and potential wildlife habitat as part of an environmental analysis. Evaluate the project site's biological conservation potential and adjoining parcels, including habitat patch size, corridors and connectivity, edge effects, and buffer potential. Evaluate cultural conditions and regional influences on the site, such as proposed adjacent developments and other potentially connecting open lands.

Identification. Determine the primary landscape functions (aesthetics, water and sediment, wildlife and plant conservation) that are important to the project area, any unique opportunities, and primary project constraints. Based on the inventory, identify landscape functions that might be needed or best expressed on the site and determine the site's overall potential as a natural ecosystem, including the opportunities and constraints of the site.

Aesthetic considerations may include the uses of tall visual screening, low visual screening, trail screening, and framing desirable views, as well as screening undesirable views, winds, or noise. Habitat considerations include allowing a movement corridor, which might include making drain culverts large enough for wildlife to pass through. Consider how wildlife will use the area for shelter, foraging, breeding areas, or migratory stopover.

Zoning. Delineate the project area into functional groups—those that have similar aesthetic needs and desires, similar water and sediment functions, and similar wildlife and animal conservation opportunities and constraints. Determine what human access will be for each zone, taking into consideration the needs of wildlife to retreat from highly impacted areas.

Design. Develop a plan which mimics the specific ecological attributes and conditions found in high-quality natural areas to achieve the landscape function and specific conservation goals desired in the project area. Mimic existing native ecosystems that are found in similar zones in Colorado.

Create opportunities for increasing diversity of plant communities where possible by altering the topography to allow for wetlands, riparian shrubs, upland shrubs, and open areas. Consider buffering high-value habitat areas with berms at an elevation that can screen wildlife from trail activities. Ideally, access by trails should not encircle the entire pond in a loop fashion unless the trail is screened or set back far enough so as not to disturb the whole shoreline for sensitive wildlife.

Buildings and homes constructed next to detention ponds and other habitats should be set back as far as possible from the open space to limit light and noise intrusion. The activities of people and associated facilities such as parking lots, public entrances, and primary doors should generally be on the opposite side from the detention ponds and other habitat areas.

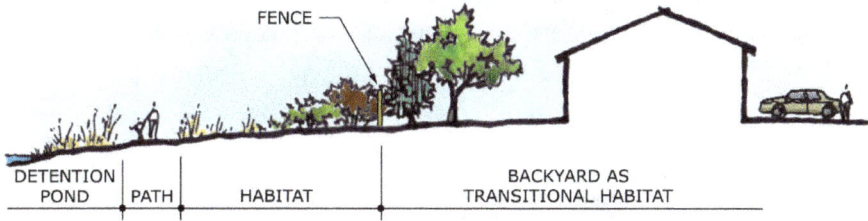

Building illustration (Courtesy of BHA Design)

Landscaping on the habitat side of buildings should consist of native plantings, to the degree possible, and provide a natural transition between the built environment, detention ponds, stream corridors, and other habitat areas. All plants included in adjacent landscapes should be evaluated for potential invasiveness.

Fallen logs, old tree trunks, or large limbs can be added to the pond to provide perching sites for birds, basking areas for reptiles and amphibians, loafing sites for waterfowl, and to add structural habitat elements to the detention basin. These need to be anchored to the bottom so that when water is in the basin, they do not float up and clog outlet structures.

High flow areas where erosion is likely, such as inlets, outlets, and stormwater conveyances, may need to be planted with wetland plugs instead of seed. Grids of string slightly above the water elevation can also be laid out across the site to prevent geese and other waterfowl from pulling up newly planted wetlands plants.

Implementation. Create a design for the project area making appropriate on-site adjustments to fit the specific site conditions. (See Seed Specifications in Chapter 11.)

After Care. Manage the project area making midcourse corrections, and adapting the design to site conditions to achieve the landscape function and conservation goals. Provide a two-year (minimum) management period. (Management strategies are discussed in Chapters 9 and 10.) Wetland vegetation must be managed to ensure that proper drainage functions are maintained.

Monitoring and Assessment. Create photo points, plots, transects, and/ or other means of collecting and tracking information about changes to the site, and feed this information back into the next phase of project management. The intention is that restoration and habitat improvement should be ongoing.

CHAPTER 14

STORMWATER PONDS

F ew applications for native grass and riparian shrubs in the built environment are more natural and beneficial than their use in vegetating stormwater ponds. When developers build rooftops, parking lots, and other impermeable surfaces, rain and snowmelt (stormwater) can no longer percolate into the ground and carry with them pollutants and nutrients. They must be managed to prevent flooding and ecological degradation downstream.

It was once common practice to collect stormwater in concrete pits and direct it into nearby rivers and streams. Over the last few decades, the standard for stormwater engineering has moved toward creating water quality ponds that slow down the turbulence of the water and allow sediment to drop out.

Ponds that include vegetation can also remove nutrients the stormwater may have picked up in its flow. These nutrients may come from natural deposition, landscape fertilizer, pet waste, soap used for washing cars, etc. Nutrients that reach ponds and lakes encourage the growth of algae, which in turn reduces oxygen levels while decaying in the water and can affect aquatic life, including fish.

Stormwater ponds, though necessary, are often viewed by developers as a liability. They can be unsightly when not well-designed, fill up with trash carried along by storm flows, and take up space that would otherwise be buildable. Remember that wetlands cover less than 2 percent of Colorado's total land area, yet more than 75 percent of wildlife species benefit from them. Well-constructed stormwater ponds can be aesthetically pleasing amenities that benefit wildlife in the built environment while offering educational and recreational opportunities for residents and visitors.

One of the most difficult things about vegetating stormwater ponds is predicting the amount of moisture the pond will hold. In the beginning, when the pond is first excavated, it may be drier. Over time, as the area around the pond gets built and runoff increases, the pond will become wetter. In dry ponds, the diverse mix listed in Chapter 4 should be used. This mix includes warm and cool-season grasses and has a broad range of moisture requirements. Ecologists prefer to use species diversity to provide stability and fill ecological niches in the environment. This diverse approach ensures that there will be some grass species in the mix that will succeed.

In general, cattails, while native, should be discouraged in wetlands and stormwater channels. Although cattails provide filtration and cover for wildlife, they are aggressive and can create a monoculture. The goal should be to create a diverse wetland plant community. When designing a pond, it is desirable to create an undulating shoreline and varying topography on the pond bottom. Shallow, flat-bottomed ponds should drain completely, or they can become a breeding ground for mosquitoes.

Ponds that have an undulating grade, and include plunge pools five feet deep or deeper, can allow minnows to survive over winter. Minnows, tadpoles, and dragonfly larvae are natural predators that can help to control mosquitoes. An undulating grade will also help to create diverse opportunities for specific planting zones within the pond including; aquatic, and flat or sloped flooded, saturated, and subirrigated zones.

Planting according to these zones can be a complicated matter and requires on-site observation by a project manager skilled in reading and interpreting the plan and making on-site adjustments. Like the grass mix mentioned previously, the following diverse wetland mix provides a wide list of species that will establish themselves where suitable conditions allow.

Wetland or Wet Meadow Areas Seed Mix, Courtesy of Western Native Seed

Seeded at a rate of 10 lbs./acre

15 % Alkali bulrush (*Bolboschoenus maritimus*)

15 % Canada wildrye (*Elymus canadensis*)

15 % Switchgrass (*Panicum virgatum)*

12 % Yellow Indiangrass (*Sorghastrum nutan*)

7 % Prairie cordgrass (*Spartina pectinate*)

6 % Nebraska sedge (*Carex nebrascensis*)

6 % Spikerush (*Eleocharis palustris*)

6 % Hardstem bulrush (*Schoenoplectus acutus*)

6 % Softstem bulrush (*Schoenoplectus tabernaemontani*)

6 % Olney's three-square bulrush (*Schoenoplectus americanus*)

4 % Baltic rush (*Juncus balticus*)

2 % Woolly sedge (*Carex pellita*)

The following tall warm-season grasses can be sown in moist low lying areas or added to the riparian wetlands mix above.

Big bluestem (*Andropogon gerardii*) "Kaw" or "Pawnee," 5 lbs.

Yellow Indiangrass (*Sorghastrum nutans*) "Tomahawk" or "Neb 54," 4 lbs.

Switchgrass (*Panicum virgatum*) "Blackwell," 1 lb.

These added to the Wet Meadow mix total 20 pounds/acre. These areas will likely be broadcast seeded and not suitable to drill seeding because of their size and/or they may be wet. To facilitate broadcasting the seed more evenly, rice hulls or sand should be added to bulk up the mix.

The Wetland Ecology Demonstration Garden at HPEC

To illustrate the distinct vegetation patterns found in each hydrological zone, we created a Wetland Ecology Demonstration Garden at HPEC in 2010. We selected an area in Old Canal Park previously disturbed and reseeded with crested wheatgrass, an invasive cool-season grass.

The spot was chosen because it needed to be restored anyway, and we were not sacrificing established native vegetation. We wanted the demonstration garden to look like a possible landform. We began by drawing out a series of channels on the ground with marking paint to create something like a braided landform akin to the shallow, meandering South Platte River.

Our garden site is bordered by an irrigation canal that had been abandoned since 1907. On the south side of the site is Equalizer Lake. Our wetland demonstration garden looks like a landform that is called a secondary channel. An ecologist looking at it might surmise that the irrigation canal overflowed periodically and created this channel draining to the lake. This doesn't actually happen, but we wanted a design that appeared to be ecologically plausible.

We brought in an excavation contractor with a backhoe and observed as they picked away at the channels painted out on the ground. Most of the channel was dug to a depth of eighteen inches. In some

Wetland Garden excavation

places, we dug five feet deep. We used the soil removed from these deeper pockets to create berms, where we added gravel and sand to create a well-drained upland zone.

Between the upland and excavated site is what is known as the subirrigated zone, a place that isn't inundated with water but has constant moisture below ground throughout the year. The shallow channels formed a wetland zone, and the deep pockets exposed the shallow groundwater to provide a place for emergent aquatic plants.

We had hoped that the excavator would be able to dig with minimal disturbance to the rest of the site. However, by the end of the project, the native grass that had existed there before was pulverized into dust. We planted piñon pine and juniper in the dry upland zone, along with rabbitbrush, big sagebrush, and dryland perennials from our nursery. Over the rest of the site, we planted grasses, sedges, and rushes arranged according to moisture requirements.

The following year we had a period of rain that lasted forty-eight hours. The excavated parts of the site filled with water, and the soil was saturated. The native grass that had been growing on the site previously began to recover and, in a short period of time, it began to fill in again. With the channels filled, the plants we installed took off and by the end of the first season. It was impossible to tell that it had ever been excavated.

The Wetland Ecology Demonstration Garden is in every sense a "garden"—a very intentional arrangement of plants driven by a specific purpose. In many ways, it is the ideal marriage of landscape design and ecological restoration. After more than a decade, the garden persists year after year with minimal care and attention. The most exciting thing about it is that it has never been watered since the initial planting, yet it is filled with interesting, thriving, and beautiful plants throughout the year. The garden has also given us wonderful surprises. Wetland wildflowers such as tulip gentian (*Eustoma grandiflorum*), marsh skullcap (*Scutellaria galericulata*), and hairy hedge nettle (*Stachys palustris var. pilosa*) showed up all on their own.

Few sounds are more evocative of spring than the sound of chorus frogs (spring peepers) in a pond at dusk. In Colorado, amphibians begin to breed not only when temperatures are warm enough, but also when there is sufficient moisture for ponds to fill. At HPEC, we have the ability to fill our stormwater pond with water from our lake. In some years, we have not been able to run the water until May or June. Within twenty-four hours of adding water, we begin to hear the chorus frogs, and within forty-eight hours, we hear the mating call of Woodhouse's toads. Because toxins flow in water to low-lying areas, amphibians are the "canary in our coal mine." Their song is more than just a lovely sound. It is a message that lets us know we're doing something right.

The concept of arranging plants in communities by their moisture requirements began to influence our thinking in everything we did. Ecological restoration and landscape design became fully fused in our minds.

In the next chapter, we explore alternative gardening styles that utilize the ecological principles discussed in the previous chapters to create ornamental landscapes that are beautiful and sustainable in the Rocky Mountain West.

Upland Zone

Wetland Ecology Demonstration Garden filled with water

Wetland Ecology Demonstration Garden

Wetland Zone

Woodhouse's toad

Old Canal Park

CHAPTER 15

DESIGNING LANDSCAPES AS ECOLOGICAL RESTORATION

Grading machines

M ore than 90 percent of the biodiversity found in a prairie is thought to be underground. The soil microbiome includes nematodes, mycorrhizae, and beneficial bacteria, which, though unseen, are essential to the ecology of grasslands. Soil structure is often damaged in the process of development. Compaction often reduces permeability and oxygen within the soil.

When a housing development is created, the soil is typically stripped off the site and piled up high where no oxygen can get into it. The pile is driven over by heavy machinery, and often weeds grow on the pile for a year or more, depositing their seeds. After the soil microbiota is long since dead, the soil is spread over individual lots where it is driven over some more by heavy machinery. After the lot is landscaped, it is saturated with irrigation water, driving even more oxygen from the soil. At this point, the homeowner might develop a complex, saying, "I can't grow anything!" or complain to their landscaper, who most likely will crank up the irrigation even more and add a lot of unnecessary chemicals.

This treatment of the soil describes the site of our visitor center. When the adjacent community center, the Lake Club, was built, our site was used as a staging area for materials and construction equipment. In the following year, we built our own building and compacted the soil even more. Although most of our site is a former farm field with the topsoil very much intact and alive, the clay soil around our building was more like concrete by the time our building project was completed.

The common wisdom about native plants is that they do not require a lot of soil prep, amendment, or nutrients. If your site is a well-drained gravelly soil near a riverbed or a mineral soil in the foothills or mountain areas, no soil amendment should be necessary. If your site is the compacted clay described above, it is necessary to break up the compaction and help to get oxygen back into the soil.

It's a matter of some debate whether or not it's beneficial to add mycorrhiza back into the soil. There are many kinds of mycorrhiza, each adapted to a specific type of plant. Our philosophy is similar to that in Chinese medicine, which says that a living organism (in this case, soil) can regulate its own health when given the proper conditions. When oxygen can permeate the soil, the microbiome will begin to recover on its own.

Adding sand to compacted clay to increase permeability only creates concrete. Organic matter is necessary to break up the clay and begin to restore soil microorganisms. We spread a mixture that is half compost and half fine gravel over our soil three inches deep and work it in as deeply as possible. It's also helpful to create raised berms to increase soil drainage for plants that thrive in high and dry environments.

Conventional landscape installations are often on a flat plane, which contradicts how plants are arranged in nature. Even on the treeless prairie, nothing is flat. When we built our visitor center, this is one

Raised berms

of the main things we wanted to share with our visitors: you can have a lush garden; you can have plantings that are dense with abundant flowers and thronging with wildlife while using little or no water to support them, if you know how.

How do you grow a wetland plant like blue vervain (*Verbena hastata*) in a garden that is never watered? It's very easy. Just plant it where the downspout deposits rainwater. This simple form of rain gardening can be applied on a microscale or to an entire landscape.

In front of our building at HPEC is a bioswale. It is a low channel that receives all of the water from our parking lot. The channel has a series of pools that are excavated to different depths. Each shallow pool contains plants with varying degrees of moisture requirements. The channel banks have plants that require increasingly less moisture up to the top of the bank, which receives virtually no moisture except our natural precipitation. This is not something that we invented. The Anasazi farmed this way over a thousand years ago in the desert Southwest, digging shallow pits to collect the scant rainfall.

This concept of passive rainwater harvesting has been implemented to a large extent in Tucson, Arizona. The story, as we've heard it, is that a landscape architect named Brad Lancaster cut into the concrete curb next to his yard. He created a shallow bowl that could collect the water

Verbena rain chain

and allow it to percolate into the ground. This created a lush oasis filled with native palo verde trees and singing birds, which became the wonder of his neighborhood.

City officials came out to write him a citation for destroying the curb. He showed them how rainwater alone supported his beautiful garden. Back at the city office, there must have been some discussions because now homeowners can apply to the city to get the curb cut to allow rainwater into their landscapes. Streets in the city of Tucson include landscaping designed to let rainwater in rather than keeping it out.

Here in Colorado, our complicated water laws do not allow for the evaporative loss of rainwater trapped in ponds of any size unless the landowner has water rights to offset it. However, it is possible to create high and low spots that allow rainwater to flow through the landscape and slow down enough to provide irrigation to the landscape before flowing on. As we mentioned in the chapter about stormwater,

Native plants in formal arrangements (*Schizachyrium scoparium, 'Standing Ovation'*)

this slows down stormwater turbulence and removes nutrient runoff, improving water quality.

At HPEC, our gardens are ablaze with color from spring until frost with virtually no watering. Our garden spans several acres, but we employ only one person as a horticulturist. We do have many volunteers who help us to weed, plant, and hand-water new plantings. Overall, our gardens are extremely low maintenance because we go with the flow of natural processes. However, there is no reason native plants cannot be used in formal designs in place of exotic species.

In some of our gardens, we deadhead, a practice intended to extend the period of bloom by preventing the plant from going to seed. However, after the middle of the summer, we stop deadheading and allow the plants to produce seed. To have a lush garden full of plants, it is necessary to allow plants to go to seed and fill in bare spots. Self-starting plants that grow from seed scattered in your garden will be much stronger than transplanted plants.

Some of our showiest plants are the ones that grow from seed scattered in the fall, including sacred datura (*Datura wrightii*), ten-petalled blazing star (*Mentzelia decapetala*), and Rocky Mountain bee plant (*Cleome serrulata*).

Sacred datura (*Datura wrightii*)

Ten-petalled blazing star (*Mentzelia decapetala*)

Rocky Mountain bee plant (*Cleome serrulata*) and two-tailed swallowtail

Brown-belted bumblebee and Maximilian sunflower (*Helianthus maximiliani*)

Ugly weed barrier

We never use weed barrier and have removed it from gardens we did not install but currently manage. Weed barrier is counter to the goals of gardening for wildlife. It creates an unnatural barrier between the world above the ground and the world below. A great many beneficial insects, worms, amphibians, and other animals need to move freely above and below ground.

Native bumble bees nest in the ground and need areas of exposed soil to survive. Weed barrier obstructs natural ecological processes, and it doesn't actually work to prevent weeds. Many weeds can grow perfectly well on top of weed barrier. Few things in the garden are uglier than exposed weed barrier when the mulch has worn away, and it's much better to go without.

In our opinion, steel edging is also used far too often and is entirely unnecessary. The logic for using steel edging seems to be keeping bed areas separated from turf areas. Rhizomatous grasses grow and spread laterally via their rhizomes—modified subterranean plant stems that send out roots and shoots. Kentucky bluegrass and buffalo grass are

Steel edging

examples of grasses that have rhizomes. Tall fescue, another popular turfgrass, does not have rhizomes; it can only spread by seeds, but conventional turf management does not allow for seed production. Commercial landscape maintenance companies typically trim the edges of beds in the course of their duties, making steel edging unnecessary.

Steel edging typically rises up at some point, becoming a distinct visual feature of the landscape and creating an unsightly safety hazard. In places where a border is required, such as the meeting of landscape beds and walking paths, we have used strip-stone edging, a much more attractive material that does not migrate out of place.

Bark mulch has its place, but that place is primarily the woodland forests of the Rocky Mountains, East Coast, and West Coast, or anywhere you can look up and see a dense canopy of trees overhead. In our experience, bark mulch is not long-lasting. In our climate, it breaks down and blows away. When used in combination with weed barrier, bark mulch slides off and seems to disappear even quicker. Another problem with bark mulch is that it encourages voles, small rodents that

Strip stone edging

will tunnel in the mulch, eating the roots of perennials and stripping the bark off of shrubs.

In terms of environmental sustainability, it's helpful to consider how far your mulch needs to travel on a truck to your site. An abundance of gravel along rivers in the Rocky Mountain West makes rock mulch a logical choice. We prefer to use a mixture of three-quarter-inch tan river rock mixed with pea stone and a kitty litter sized rock called squeegee mixed in equal portions. The mixed sizes of material create a natural look that resembles the appearance of the ground in natural areas.

Testing conducted by our friends at Northern Water (the headquarters of the Northern Colorado Water Conservancy District) in Berthoud, Colorado, reveal that the temperature on top of rock is much hotter in the day than on top of bark mulch, but that is appropriate for native plants adapted to this climate. Under the rock however, the soil temperature remains the same as under mulch. Another advantage of

Mixed rock mulch

rock mulch is that it does not hold on to moisture the way that bark does. When trace amounts of rain falls, moisture can adhere to mulch and simply evaporate, whereas moisture passes quickly through rock to reach the plant's roots. One more advantage of rock is that it provides an ideal medium for native plant seedlings to get started.

When we think about our landscape as an ecological restoration, every part of our site is regarded as a microclimate. Microclimates can be as small as from one side of a boulder to the other. One side may be hot, the other side shady, therefore different opportunities exist within this small area. When we get used to this concept, it's easy to see why plants may thrive in one spot but cannot survive in another just a few feet away.

Ecologists look at the aspect (the direction the site faces and the amount of sunlight it receives) as well as the degree of slopes, variations in soil moisture, and other conditions of the site. All of this is applicable even in the smallest home landscaping project. Spots surrounding buildings receive different amounts of stormwater, sunlight, exposure to wind, and other influences. To create a low maintenance native garden, it is necessary to evaluate the site in these terms and put the right plant in the right place for our purposes.

The following table will provide information on site evaluation, plant characteristics, and wildlife benefits.

Bioswale at HPEC - September

Bioswale at HPEC - June

Common Name	Latin Name	Height	Width	Exposure
Shrubs and trees for "Mesic" (moist not saturated) areas				
Rocky Mountain Maple	Acer glabrum	10' - 30'	10' - 15'	Full sun
Bigtooth Maple	Acer grandidentatum	10' - 30'	20' - 30'	Full sun
Box Elder	Acer negundo	25'-30'	20'-25'	Full sun
Thinleaf Alder	Alnus incana ssp. tenuifolia	15' -40'	15' -40'	Full sun/ pt. shade
Saskatoon Serviceberry	Amelanchier alnifolia	4' - 15'	6' - 8'	Full sun /pt. shade
Shadblow Serviceberry	Amelanchier canadensis	25'-30'	20'-25'	Full sun /pt. shade
River Birch	Betula occidentalis	25'-30'	20'-25'	Full sun /pt. shade
Shiny-leaved Hawthorn	Crataegus erythropoda	10' - 20'	8' - 15'	Sun/pt. shade
Western Chokecherry	Prunus virginiana var. melanocarpa	15' - 25'	10' - 15'	Sun/pt. shade
Blue Spruce	Picea pungens	50' - 80'	10' - 25'	Sun/ pt. shade
	(mesa verde)			
Quaking Aspen	Populus tremuloides	30' - 50'	clump	Full sun
Shrubby Cinquefoil	Potentilla fruticosa (Pentaphylloides floribunda)	3' - 4'	2' - 3'	Full sun

Characteristics & notes	Wildlife Value
Large shrub, inconspicuous flowers	Shelter for birds
Small tree, inconspicuous flowers	Shelter for birds
Large shrub or small tree, inconspicuous flowers	Attracts birds, honey bees, and other insects including the boxelder beetle
Large multi-stem shrub, catkins	Seeds and buds provide winter food for birds
White flowers in spring, berries in June	Flowers for butterflies, berries for birds and mammals, shelter for birds
White flowers in spring, berries in June. Name comes from the coastal upstream breeding migration of the Shad (fish) which coincides with the bloom of this shrub	Flowers for butterflies, berries for birds and mammals, shelter for birds
Interesting bark, flowers are "catkins" dense, elongated, and drooping cluster of flowers without petals.	As a wind pollinated plant river birch does not attract pollinators, seeds provide forage for birds in winter
White flowers spring, persistent red berries	Attracts native bees and other insects; berries are eaten by birds
White flowers spring, followed by cluster of small dark purple fruit; can sucker especially in moist soils	Attracts bees and butterflies such as western tiger swallowtail, two-tailed swallowtail,; fruit for birds
Evergreen foliage blue to green	Shelter and seeds for birds and squirrels. Favorite nesting and roosting spots for great horned owls
Clump forming, fall foliage ranges from gold to orange	Shelter for birds, grouse & quail eat winter buds; attracts butterflies- larval host for Eastern Tiger Swallowtail & Viceroy
Yellow flowers bloom continually summer to fall	Nectar & pollen for small generalist pollinators; attracts butterflies & native bees

Common Name	Latin Name	Height	Width	Exposure
Wild Plum	Prunus americana	12 - 20'	12 - 20'	Sun/ pt. shade
Western Sand Cherry	Prunus pumila var. besseyi	2' - 6'	2' - 4'	Sun/ pt. shade
Wax Currant	Ribes cereum	3' - 4'	3' - 4'	Sun/ pt. shade
Golden Elderberry	Sambucus canadensis 'aurea'	8' - 12'	4' - 8'	Sun/ pt. shade
Shrubs for subirrigated areas				
Leadplant; False Indigo	Amorpha fruticosa	6' - 12'	4' - 6'	Sun/ pt. shade
Red Twig Dogwood	Cornus sericea	15'	15'	Sun/ pt. shade
Twinberry Honeysuckle	Lonicera involucrata	6'- 10'	4' - 8"	Sun/ pt. shade
Plains Cottonwood	Populus deltoides	75'- 100'	50' - 75'	Full sun
Ribes americanum	Ribes aureum	4' - 6'	4' - 6'	Sun/ pt. shade
American Black Currant		2' - 4'	2' - 4'	Sun/ pt. shade

Characteristics & notes	Wildlife Value
White flowers appear before foliage in early spring. Edible fruits develop in late summer.	Nectar and pollen for native bees, bumblebees, & honey bees; nesting cover and fruit for birds and other wildlife; host plant for many butterfly species.
White flowers in spring, purple black berries; toxic- do not eat!	Nectar and pollen for bees; fruit for birds and other wildlife
Pinkish-white flowers, late spring	Nectar and pollen for many pollinators; fruit for birds and other wildlife; provides shelter & cover; attracts native bees; provides some of the earliest nectar for pollinators
Flat topped white flower cluster followed by blue of purple berries	Fruit eaten by birds
Purple flowers summer	Nectar and pollen for bees & butterflies; larval host for moths- dogfaces, silver-spotted skipper, gray hairstreak, & hoary edge skipper; Mammals including deer attracted to fruit
White flowers & berries; red twigs provide good winter interest	Shelter for small mammals birds- waterfowl, marsh, & shorebirds; deer forage; attracts birds & butterflies; larval host for spring azure moth
Yellow flowers in spring ripen into (inedible) purple berries mid summer	Attracts hummingbirds. Fruit eaten by songbirds
Large tree found along prairie watersheds. Inconspicuous flowers	Shelter & food for birds and other wildlife; host for mourning cloak, red-spotted purple, viceroy, & tiger swallowtail butterflies
Bright yellow flowers appear in early spring, some are clove scented, edible fruit is yellow, red or purple, attractive red foliage in fall. this plant prefers a wet environment but is adaptable to dryer sites	Birds & mammals feed on berries-bears, raccoons, mice; attracts native pollinators, specifically bumble bees, butterflies, & moths
White flowers, black fruits, red fall foliage	Birds & mammals feed on berries-bears, raccoons, mice; attracts native pollinators, specifically bumble bees, butterflies, & moths

Common Name	Latin Name	Height	Width	Exposure
Gooseberry	Ribes inerme	2' - 4'	2' - 4'w	Sun/ pt. shade
Peachleaf Willow	Salix amygdaloides (small tree)	20' - 40'	40'	Sun/ pt. shade

Shrubs for Wetland areas				
Sandbar/Coyote Willow	Salix exigua	5' - 20'	clump	Sun/ pt. shade
Bluestem Willow	Salix irrorata	5' - 8'	4' - 6'	Sun/ pt. shade

Shrubs and Trees for Dry Sites - North and East Facing				
Utah Serviceberry	Amelanchier utahensis	12' - 15'	12'	Sun/ pt. shade
Silvery Leadplant	Amorpha canescens	2' - 4'	2' - 4'	Full sun
Greenleaf Manzanita	Arctostaphylos patula	1' - 6'	8'	Full sun
Kinnikinic	Arctostaphylos uva-ursi	1'	5'	Sun/ pt. shade
Netleaf Hackberry	Celtis reticulata (Small Tree)	10' - 15'	8' - 12'	Sun/ pt. shade
Mountain Mahogany	Cercocarpus montanus	5' - 10'	4' - 6'	Sun/ pt. shade

Characteristics & notes	Wildlife Value
Thorny stems, flower whitish/pink, purple fruit	Birds that eat gooseberries, include catbirds, thrashers, robins, and waxwings
Reddish flowers (catkins) in spring, gold leaves in fall	Nesting site & material for birds; mammals & birds eat seeds; attracts butterflies- larval host to Mourning Cloak & Viceroy as well as two-tailed swallowtails, & western tiger swallowtail; attracts native bees
Yellow catkins in spring; stream stabilization, spreads aggressively which makes it undesirable for some landscapes	Provides cover and nesting for birds and other wildlife. Attracts native bees & birds; supports Rocky Mtn. Agapema moth
Yellow catkins spring, bluish twigs; showy all 4 seasons	Attracts native bees
White , spring	Berries for birds and other wildlife- mammals & birds forage & eat fruit; nectar for pollinators - native bees
Violet-purple, midsummer	Nectar and pollen for bees & butterflies; mammals including deer attracted to fruit
White to Pink, Spring, broadleaf evergreen, benefits from protection from wind particularly in winter, will not tolerate saturated soil; many cultivated varieties are selected for low growing characteristics	Pollen and nectar for bees, fruit for birds and other wildlife
Pink flowers, early summer, small mealy red fruit in fall, broadleaf evergreen	Pollen and nectar for bees; fruit for birds, bears, & small mammals; attracts bees, hummingbirds & butterflies- larval host to Hoary & Brown Elfin, Feija Fritillary
Inconspicuous flowers spring	Attracts birds & butterflies like the hackberry butterfly; fruit eaten by wildlife & birds
White flowers in spring, interesting spiraled seeds in late summer	Shelter for birds; attracts butterflies & moths

Common Name	Latin Name	Height	Width	Exposure
Mountain Spray	Holodiscus dumosus	4' - 7'	5'	Sun/ pt. shade
Common Juniper	Juniperus communis	1'	6' - 12'	Sun/ pt. shade
Creeping Mahonia	Mahonia repens	1'	1'	Sun/ pt. shade
Lewis Mock Orange	Philadelphus lewisii	5' - 10'	5' - 10'	Sun/ pt. shade
Mountain Ninebark	Physocarpus monogynus	5' - 8'	4' - 6'	Sun/pt. shade
Gambel Oak	Quercus gambelii	25'	12'	Full sun
Smooth Sumac	Rhus glabra cismontana	8-12'	6'	Sun/pt. shade
Staghorn Sumac	Rhus typhinia	15' - 25-	20' - 30'	Sun/pt. shade
Boulder raspberry	Rubus (Oreobatus) deliciosus	4'	4'	Sun/pt. shade
Wood's Rose	Rosa woodsii	2' - 6'	3' - 6'	Sun/pt. shade
Western Snowberry	Symphoricarpos occidentalis	2' - 3'	4' - 8'	Sun/pt. shade

Characteristics & notes	Wildlife Value
Cream colored flower sprays, midsummer	Forage/browse for wildlife
Low spreading evergreen	Provide edible fruit and dense nesting sites for birds
Broadleaf evergreen, yellow flowers in spring, ornamental blue fruit.	Nectar and pollen for bees and butterflies; cover for wildlife; attracts birds & native bees
Large fragrant white flowers early summer	Forage for bees and generalist pollinators, nesting sites for birds
Clusters of small white flowers in mid summer followed by attractive fruit	Forage for bees and generalist pollinators, nesting sites for birds
Inconspicuous flowers, dried leaves persist until spring	Acorns & nesting site for birds and other wildlife; host for Colorado hairstreak butterfly larva; provides food & cover for deer & small mammals; Host plant for Colorado hairstreak butterfly
Shiny, dark green foliage, inconspicuous green flowers; this plant can spread aggressively - good for bank stabilization	Shelter and food for birds & small mammals; food for deer; attracts bees, birds & butterflies- larval host for Hairstreak butterfly
Red seed clusters reminiscent of antlers, foliage turns brilliant red in fall, spreads aggressively	Ring-necked pheasant, bobwhite quail, wild turkey, and about 300 species of songbirds include sumac fruit in their diet. It is also know to be important only in the winter diets of ruffed grouse and the sharp-tailed grouse.
White, early summer; berries unpalatable	Nectar, pollen, & nesting materials for bees; fruit for birds and other wildlife
Highly fragrant pink flowers in late spring, red hips persist in winter; can sucker, especially in moist soils	Nectar, pollen, & nesting materials for bees; fruit for birds, and other wildlife
White flowers & berries spring; toxic if eaten by humans	Food, cover, & nesting for birds, small mammals, attracts hummingbirds & bees

Common Name	Latin Name	Height	Width	Exposure
Shrubs, Trees, etc. for Hot, Dry Sites - South and West Facing				
New Mexico Hardy Century Plant	Agave neomexicana subsp. parryi	1'	1'	Full sun
Desert False Indigo	Amorpha canecens	1' - 3'	1' - 3'	Full sun
Dwarf Indigo Bush	Amorpha nana	2' - 3'	2' - 3'	Full sun
Silver Sage	Artemisia cana	3' - 4'	3' - 4'	Full sun
Sand Sagebrush	Artemisia filifolia (Oligoporus filifolius)	3' - 4'	3' - 4'	Full sun
Sagebrush	Artemisia tridentata	1' - 5'	2' - 3'	Full sun
Four wing Saltbush	Atriplex canescens	2' - 6'	3' - 8'	Full sun
Littleleaf Mtn. Mahogany	Cercocarpus ledifolius var. intricatus	3' - 5-	2' - 3'	Full sun
Curl Leaf Mtn. Mahogany	Curl Leaf Mountain Mahogany	10'- 30'	10" - 12"	Full sun
Fernbush	Chamaebatiaria millefolium	4' - 6'	4' - 6'	Full sun
Cliffrose	Cowania (Purshia) stansburyana			Full sun
Cholla	Cylindropuntia imbricata	6' - 4'	3'	Full sun
Rubber Rabbitbrush	Ericameria (Chrysothamnus) nauseosus	4' - 6'	4' - 6'	Full sun

Characteristics & notes	Wildlife Value
Spikey gray green foliage, mature plants send up a 1o foot tall spike of yellow flowers.	Hummingbirds
Gray foliage, purple flowers summer	Nectar and pollen for bees & butterflies
Blue flower spike in mid summer	Bees and butterflies are attracted to the sweet smelling blossoms, host plant for the larvae of the native Silver Spotted Skipper butterfly
Silver gray foliage	Low pollinator interest
Silver gray foliage	Pollen & nesting materials/site for native bees; shelter and food for birds- sharp-tail grouse
Silver gray foliage	Nectar, pollen, and nesting materials and structure for native bees; attracts birds & butterflies
Gray foliage, interesting 4 chambered fruits develop in late summer and persist into winter	Cover & food for mammals & birds; nectar & pollen for pollinating insects; toxic to livestock (selenium)
Interesting form is often ruined by over-pruning. Evergreen foliage	The dense branching habit offers excellent cover for songbirds year-round, and the small, flowers that appear for two to three weeks are an excellent source of nectar for bees in spring.
Evergreen shrub	
White, summer	Attracts bees, butterflies, pollinating insects; larval host for spring azure butterfly
White flowers	Seeds provide food for song birds
Cactus, magenta flowers in late spring	Nectar and pollen for bees; fruit for birds and other wildlife
Silver green with yellow flowers late summer	Nectar & pollen for many pollinators; host plant for checkerspot butterfly larva, small bees and migrating painted ladies

Common Name	Latin Name	Height	Width	Exposure
Mormon Tea	Ephedra viridis	3' - 6'	2' - 5'	Full sun
Apache Plume	Fallugia paradoxa	5' - 8'	3' - 6'	Full sun
Cliff Fendler Bush	Fendlera rupicola	4' - 6'	2' - 3'	Full sun
Single-leaf Ash	Fraxinus anomala	12' - 36'	12'	Full sun
Fremont Mahonia	Mahonia (berberis) fremontii	6' - 10'	4' - 6'	Full sun
Littleleaf Mock Orange	Philadelphus microphylus	3' - 6'	3' - 6'	Full sun
Pawnee Buttes Sandcherry	Prunus besseyii 'Pawnee Buttes'	2'	5'	Full sun
Wafer Ash	Ptelea trifoliata	15' - 25'		Full sun
Oneseed Juniper	Juniperus monosperma	8' - 20'	12'	Full sun
Rocky Mountain Juniper	Juniperus scopulorum	12' -36'	12'	Full sun
Winterfat	Krascheninnikovia lanata	1' - 2'	1' - 2'	Full sun
Squaw Apple	Peraphyllum ramosissimum	6' - 10'	4' - 8'	Full sun
Pinon Pine	Pinus edulis	20' - 30'	12' - 18'	Full sun
Ponderosa Pine	Pinus ponderosa	80'- 100'	20' - 40'	Full sun
Wavy Oak	Quercus undulata	4' - 10'	4' - 10'	Full sun

Characteristics & notes	Wildlife Value
Inconspicuous flowers, dark green twig-like foliage	Low pollinator interest
White flowers and fluffy seed, summer	Attracts native bees
Creamy white flowers, fruits remain on the plant for a long time	Forage for wildlife; cover, nesting, nectar & pollen for insects
Inconspicuous flowers	Host plant for swallowtail butterfly larva
Broadleaf evergreen, pale yellow flowers in spring, red berries.	Fruit provides forage for songbirds
Fragrant white or cream flowers early summer	Attracts birds and native bees
Low spreading Prunus besseyii cultivar, Will not tolerate over watering	Nesting spots, fruit or seeds for songbirds, nectar for pollinators.
Wafer-like papery seeds, foliage has a "skunky" smell	Host and nectar plant for butterflies and moths
Large evergreen shrub	Shelter and seeds for birds
Evergreen foliage ranges from blue to green, attactive blue fruit, many cultivars have been introduced into the nursery trade	Cover, nesting site, food for small mammals and birds: Cedar waxwings, northern mockingbird, evening grosbeak; attracts butterflies; larval host for olive butterfly
Silvery gray foliage, inconspicuous flower spring	Shelter and seeds for birds
This rare and unusual shrubs bears the typical five-petaled white flowers of the rose family, followed by a medium sized fruit resembling an apple	Fruit eaten by birds
Short needled evergreen, source of edible "pine nuts"	Seeds for birds and other wildlife
Evergreen, extreme damage has been noted in irrigated ponderosa pines after sudden fall freezes, keep dry	Seeds, nesting and perching for birds, seeds for small mammals
These scrubby oaks hybridize easily their semi-evergreen leaves have a wide range of shapes	Provide shelter and forage for a wide range of birds

Common Name	Latin Name	Height	Width	Exposure
Three-leaved Sumac	Rhus trilobata	3' - 6'	4' - 8'	Full sun
Banana Yucca	Yucca bacatta	2'	1.5'	Full sun
Soaptree Yucca	Yucca elata	8' - 12'	6'- 8'	Full sun
Plains Yucca	Yucca glauca	2' - 3'	2' - 3'	Full sun
Narrow Leaf Yucca	Yucca harrimaniae	1' - 3'	1' - 2'	Full sun
Grasses for Dry Sites				
Indian Rice Grass	Achnatherum (Oryzopsis) hymenoides	18"	18"	Full sun
Silver Bluestem	Bothriochloa laguroides	48"	24"	Full sun
Side Oats Grama	Bouteloua curtipendula	24"	18"	Full sun
Blue Grama	Bouteloua gracilis	12"-16"	8"- 12"	Full sun
Buffalo Grass	Buchloe dactyloides	8"	Spreading	Full sun
Green Needlegrass	Nassella viridula		Spreading	Full sun
Western Wheatgrass	Pascopyrum smithii	12"- 18"	Spreading	Full sun

Characteristics & notes	Wildlife Value
Orange-red berries summer/fall. Leaves are highly fragrant with a slightly "skunky" smell. Red fall foliage,	food, shelter, & nesting for gamebirds, songbirds, and mammals; nesting value for native bees
White flower spikes in early summer. Attractive, evergreen leaves are extremely sharp	Native from southeastern California north to Utah, east to western Texas and south to Sonora and Chihuahua. Few if any pollinators noted outside it's native range
Tree-like yucca plant. Native to western Texas, New Mexico, Arizona, southern Nevada, southwestern Utah, and northern Mexico. Not hardy in high altitude sites or north of Denver.	Few if any pollinators noted outside it's native range
Tall white flower stalks, late spring	Food & nesting for birds, reptiles, and small mammals; attracts bees & butterflies; larval host for yucca moth
White, summer	Food & nesting for birds, reptiles, and small mammals; attracts bees & butterflies; larval host for yucca moth
Warm season, bunchgrass	Seeds & forage for birds & small wildlife; attracts butterflies; host for green skipper larvae
Warm season, bunchgrass	Forage for wildlife and birds; attracts butterflies; host for green skipper & satyrs larvae
Warm season, bunchy sod forming	Food, nesting, & cover for birds; forage for mammals; attracts bees & butterflies; host for green skipper & dotted skipper larvae
Warm season, bunchy sod forming	Seeds for birds; grazing for wildlife; attracts butterflies & moths- host for green skipper larvae
Warm season, sod forming, suitable for turfgrass.	Forage & winter browse for mammals; Seeds & nesting materials for birds; attracts butterflies- host for green skipper larvae
Cool season, bunchgrass	Food & Cover for birds
Cool season, sod forming	Attracts birds- food & cover

Common Name	Latin Name	Height	Width	Exposure
Little Bluestem	Schizachyrium scoparium	1' - 4'	1.5'	Full sun
Sand Dropseed	Sporobolus cryptandrus	2' - 3'	1.5'	Full sun
Prairie Dropseed	Sporobolus heterolepsis	2 to 2.12	1.5'	Full sun
Grasses for Subirrigated Areas				
Big Bluestem	Andropogon gerardii	48"	24"	Sun/pt. shade
Canada Wild Rye	Elymus canadensis	24"- 36"	Spreading	Sun/pt. shade
Switchgrass	Panicum virgatum	48"	24'	Sun/pt. shade
Nuttall Alkaligrass	Puccinellia nuttaliana	12" - 18"	12" - 18"	Sun/pt. shade
Yellow Indiangrass	Sorghastrum nutans	48"	24"	Sun/pt. shade
Alkali Sacaton	Sporobolus airoides	24"	18"	Sun/pt. shade
Grass (like) Species for Wetland Areas				
Prairie Cordgrass	Spartina pectinata	48"	Spreading	Sun/pt. shade

Characteristics & notes	Wildlife Value
Warm season, bunchgrass	Seeds & cover for birds; forage, nesting material, and cover for small mammals; attracts bees & butterflies- larval host for green, Indian, crossline, Otoe, dixie, & dusted skippers, & cobwed butterfly; reddish fall color
Warm season, bunchgrass	Nesting material & cover for native bees; seeds for birds- quail
Warm season, bunchgrass	Nesting material & cover for native bees; Seeds for birds; attracts butterflies- larval host for skippers
Warm season, bunchgrass	Nesting, Cover, & food for many birds- Grasshopper, Henslow's, & other sparrows, Sedge Wrens, Western Meadowlarks, and others; attracts bees and butterflies- larval host for Delaware & Dusted skippers
Cool season, short-lived bunchgrass	Food & Nesting materials for birds; forage for small mammals; attracts butterflies- larval host for zabulon skipper
Warm season, bunchgrass	Attracts birds- food, cover, and nesting materials; attracts butterflies- larval host for Delaware skipper, and most banded skippers and satyr butterflies
Cool season, bunchgrass - salt tolerance makes this plant a good choice for rain gardens	Forage and cover for wildlife waterfowl
Warm season, bunchgrass	Seeds & nesting materials for birds; food for small mammals; attracts butterflies- larval host for pepper & salt skipper
Cool season, Bunchgrass	Nesting materials for native bees
Warm season, sod forming, blades can be razor sharp	Food, nesting, & cover for small mammals & wetland birds- Canada goose, mallard ducks, other ducks

Common Name	Latin Name	Height	Width	Exposure
Inland Saltgrass	Distichlis spicata	0.5 to1.5	Spreading	Sun/pt. shade
Fowl Bluegrass	Poa palustris	1 to1.5	1 to1.5	Sun/pt. shade
Nebraska Sedge	Carex nebrascensis	1 to 2.5	Spreading	Sun/pt. shade
Woolly Sedge	Carex pellita	1 to 3	Spreading	Sun/pt. shade
Creeping Spikerush	Eleocharis palustris	0.5 to 2	Spreading	Sun/ pt. shade
Torrey's Rush	Juncus torreyi	1 to 2.5	Spreading	Sun/ pt. shade
Baltic Rush	Juncus balticus	0.5 to 2.5	Spreading	Sun/ pt. shade

Flowering Plants for Wetland Areas				
Swamp Milkweed	Asclepias incarnata	24"-36"	24"-36"	Sun/ pt. shade
Nuttall's Sunflower	Helianthus nuttallii		36" - 70"	Sun/ pt. shade
Blue Vervain	Verbena hastata	24" - 48"	18" - 36"	Sun/ pt. shade
Tulip Gentian	Eustoma grandiflorum	10" - 15"	6"	Sun
Emergent Grass (like) Species for Aquatic Areas				
American Three-square	Schoenoplectus pungens	2 to 4	Spreading	Sun/ pt. shade

Characteristics & notes	Wildlife Value
Warm season, sod forming	Attracts birds & butterflies- larval host for sandhill and other skippers
Cool season, Bunchgrass	Provides food and cover for waterfowl
Cool season, sod forming	Forage for waterfowl
Cool season, sod forming	Food for small mammals and wetland birds- geese, waterfowl; Attracts butterflies- larval host for skippers
Cool season, sod forming	Grazed by big game animals; food, cover, and nesting for waterfowl- ducks & geese
Cool season, sod forming	Cover & food for small mammals & birds- ducks, geese, other waterfowl
Cool season, sod forming, helps to bind wetland soils	Baltic Rush and similar plants provide nesting habitat for ducks and other wetland birds; the Yellow Rail uses the stems of Baltic Rush in the construction of its nests. Dense stands of Baltic Rush and similar plants provide protective cover in wetlands for small birds and other kinds of wildlife.
Deep pink late summer	Nectar and pollen for many pollinators such as butterflies; host plant for monarch larva
Yellow late summer, fall	Food & cover for small mammals & birds; Attracts butterflies like the gorgone' checkerspot & bees
Bluish purple, late summer	Attracts birds, bees, & butterflies- larval host for common buckeye
Purple, mid to late summer	
Sod forming	Food, forage, cover, & nesting for small mammals and wetland birds- geese, ducks, wrens, blackbirds, snipes, moorhens, others

Common Name	Latin Name	Height	Width	Exposure
Smallfruit Bulrush	Scirpus microcarpus	1 to 3	Spreading	Sun/ pt. shade
Pale Bulrush	Scirpus pallidus	1 to 3	Spreading	Sun/ pt. shade
Softstem Bulrush	Schoenoplectus tabernaemontani	2 to 4	Spreading	Sun/ pt. shade
Hardstem Bulrush	Schoenoplectus acutus	2 to 4	Spreading	Sun/ pt. shade
Giant Burreed	Sparganium eurycarpum	2 to 4	Spreading	Sun/ pt. shade

Flowering Plants for Aquatic Areas (Emergent)				
Spatterdock	Nuphar lutea	0"	Spreading	Full sun
Broadleaf Arrowhead	Sagittaria latifolia		Spreading	Full sun
Flowering Perennials (Forbs) for Native Gardens				
Yarrow	Achillea millefolium L.	24"	18"	Full sun
Hummingbird Mint	Agastache rupestris			Full sun
Anise Hyssop	Agastache foeniculum			Full sun
Nettle-Leaf Hyssop	Agastache urticifolia			Full sun
Nodding Onion	Allium cernuum	10"	6"	Full sun
Jones' Bluestar	Amsonia jonesii	18"	18"	Full Sun

Characteristics & notes	Wildlife Value
Sod forming	Food, shelter, & nesting materials for small mammals & birds
Sod forming	Food & cover for small mammals & birds-waterfowl, ducks
Sod forming	Food & cover for small mammals & birds-waterfowl, ducks
Sod forming	Food & cover for small mammals & birds-waterfowl, ducks; forage for large game if food is scarce
Sod forming	Food & cover for small mammals & wetland birds- sandhill crane, American coot, king rail, various ducks; forage for white tailed deer
Yellow waterlily	Greatly improves habitat for fish breeding. Helps to reduce algae, provides food for aquatic animals- snails, fish, insects, painted turtles & snapping turtles
Arrow shaped leaf white flower	known as "duck potatoes- eaten by waterfowl, turtles, & muskrats.
White, midsummer	Nectar and pollen for generalist pollinators- specifically native bees
Orange flowers mid to late summer	Forage for hummingbirds and bees
Purple flowers mid to late summer	Forage for hummingbirds and bees
White flowers	Milbert's Tortoishell, monarch butterfly, hummingbirds, moths and a nectar-beaing plant for bees
Pink, summer	Nectar and pollen for generalist pollinators
White to blue, late spring to mid-summer	Nectar and pollen for generalist pollinators

Common Name	Latin Name	Height	Width	Exposure
Pearly Everlasting	Anaphalis margaritacea	18"	18"	Full sun
Canada Anemone	Anemone canadensis	10" - 12"	Spreading	Full sun/pt. shade
Cut-leaved Windflower	Anemone multifida	12" - 18"	Spreading	Full sun/pt. shade
Small Leaf Pussytoes	Antennaria plantaginifolia	6"	12"	Full sun
Crested Pricklypoppy	Argemone polyanthemos	36"	24"	Full sun
Fringed Sage	Artemisia frigida	12"	12"	Full sun
Prairie Sage	Artemisia ludoviciana	18" - 36"	Spreading	Full sun
Red Columbine	Aquilegia canadensis	16"	12"	Sun/pt. shade
Blue Columbine	Aquilegia caerulea	12"	12"	Sun/pt. shade
Yellow Columbine	Aquilegia chrysantha	18"	18"	Sun/pt. shade
Rose Milkweed	Asclepias incarnata	12"	36"	Full sun
Showy Milkweed	Asclepias speciosa	30"	24"	Sun/ pt. shade

Characteristics & notes	Wildlife Value
White, midsummer	Nectar and pollen for generalist pollinators; host for Painted Lady & Skipper Butterflies; silvery foliage; excellent dried flower
White flowers in spring, can spread aggressively, good as groundcover	Generalist pollinators
Creamy-white flowers in spring, can spread aggressively, good as groundcover	Generalist pollinators
White, midsummer - early fall	Nectar and pollen for small generalist pollinators; attracts Painted Lady Butterflies; gray-blue foliage, well-drained soils
Large showy white flowers in summer. Stalk is prickly to the touch. Sap can be mildly irritating	Attracts bees and beetles
Deeply cut silvery foliage, flowers pale yellow and inconspicuous	Wind pollinated, low attraction for pollinators
Fragrant silvery foliage, flowers pale yellow and inconspicuous	
Red flowers with yellow interior early summer	Nectar and pollen for bumblebees, butterflies and hummingbirds
Blue/purple and white, early summer	Nectar and pollen for bumblebees, butterflies and hummingbirds. Colorado State flower. Name comes from the Latin Aquila- Eagle, spurs resemble Eagle talons
Yellow flowers bloom continually summer to fall	Nectar and pollen for bumblebees, butterflies and hummingbirds
Perhaps the best milkweed for gardens, this plant behaves like typical landscape plants, remaining neat and tidy without moving from the spot where it was planted. Requires moisture.	Nectar and pollen for native insect pollinators, specifically native bees, butterflies, & hummingbirds; host plant for Monarch Butterfly larva.
Pink, summer, can appear "rangy" in garden. This milkweed will roam around.	Nectar and pollen for native insect pollinators, specifically native bees, butterflies, & hummingbirds; host plant for Monarch Butterfly larva.

Common Name	Latin Name	Height	Width	Exposure
Horsetail Milkweed	Asclepias subverticilata	24"	24"	Full sun
Butterfly Milkweed	Asclepias tuberosa	18"	18"	Full sun
Drummond's Milkvetch	Astragalus drummondii			Full sun
Arrowleaf Balsamroot	Balsamorhiza sagittata	12" - 18"	12" - 18"	Full sun
Chocolate Flower	Berlandiera lyrata	18"	24"	Full sun
Mariposa Lilly	Calachortus gunnsonii	12" -18"	6"	Full sun
Wine Cups	Callirhoe involucrata	12"	36"	Full sun
Sundrops	Calylophus serrulatus	12"	12"	Full sun
Harebell	Campanula rotundifolia	8"	12"	Full sun
Partridge Pea	Chamaecrista fasciculata	24"	12"	Full sun
Western Virgin's Bower	Clematis ligusticistylus			Sun/ pt. shade
Sugarbowls Clematis	Clematis scottii	12"	18"	
Rocky Mountain Beeplant	Cleome serrulata	35"	12"	Full sun
Lanceleaved Coreopsis	Coreopsis lanceolata	12"-18"	12"-18"	Full sun

Characteristics & notes	Wildlife Value
White flowers are extremely long blooming. Re-seeds and spreads readily.	Appears to attract native wasps
Orange, showy! Summer blooming. This milkweed can tolerate moderately dry sites.	Nectar and pollen for native insect pollinators, specifically native bees, butterflies, & hummingbirds; host plant for Monarch & Hairstreak Butterfly & Queen Moth larva.
Creamy white flowers bloom in early summer	Pollinated by a wide variety of bumble bee species
Yellow flowers in early summer. Native to moist, montane meadows	Generalist pollinators
Yellow, summer, smells like chocolate on summer mornings	Nectar and pollen for small generalist pollinators
White flowers in spring	Attracts bees, wasps, bee flies, and beetles.
Magenta, early summer to fall	Nectar and pollen for small generalist pollinators, specifically native bees & butterflies- host for Fritillary & Gray Hairstreak butterflies
Yellow, late spring to mid summer	Nectar and pollen for native bees
Blue, mid to late spring	Nectar and pollen for native bees & hummingbirds; moist soils; circumpolar (found at the same latitude across the globe)
Yellow annual flowers, prefer to grow in well dry	Bumble bees, larval host for the Little Yellow, Sleepy Orange and Orange Sulfur butterflies.
Vine - White flower in late summer	Attract bees
Purple, spring to early summer	Nectar and pollen for bees and butterflies
Flowers light purple to pink bloom mid summer to fall - Self-seeding annual	Attracts a large number of bees, butterflies, and hummingbirds
Yellow flowers mid summer to fall	A digger bee, Melissodes coreopsis, is an oligolege (specialist pollinator) of Coreopsis spp.

Common Name	Latin Name	Height	Width	Exposure
Plains Coreopsis	Coreopsis tinctoria	Full sun	12"	Full sun
White Prairie Clover	Dalea candida	18"	12"	Full sun
Purple Prairie Clover	Dalea purpurea	18"	12"	Full sun
Sacred Datura	Datura wrightii	30"	36"	Full sun
Shooting Star	Dodecatheon pulchellum	8"	6"	Sun/pt. shade
Narrowleaf Coneflower	Echinacea angustifolia	12" - 18"	12"	Full sun
Pale Coneflower	Echinacea pallida	18" - 24"	12" to 18"	Full sun
Bush's Coneflower	Echinacea paradoxa	24" - 36"	24"	Full sun
Purple Coneflower	Echinacea purperea	18" - 24"	18"	Full sun
Engelmann Daisy	Engelmannia peristenia	18" 36"	15" - 18"	Full sun
Scarlet Hedgehog Cactus	Echinocereus coccineus	6"	12"	Sun/ pt. shade
Claret Cup Cactus	Echinocereus triglochidiatus	12"	18"	Full sun
Engleman Daisy	Engelmannia peristenia	24"	18"	Full sun
Fernleaf Fleabane	Erigeron compositus	6"	6"	Full sun
Trailing Fleabane	Erigeron flagellaris	6"	18"	Full sun
Showy Daisy, Fleabane	Erigeron speciosus	24"	18"	Sun/ pt. shade

Characteristics & notes	Wildlife Value
Yellow flowers with dark red center - Annual	
White to blue, late spring to mid-summer	Nectar and pollen for native bees and butterflies
Purple, summer; fixes nitrogen and can improve soil fertility	Nectar and pollen for native bees and butterflies
Large self-seeding annual bearing large white to pale violet flowers mid to late summer	Attract small native bees
Small, deep pink flowers bloom in summer. Requires ample moisture	Pollinated by bees
Deep pink, mid to late summer	Attract bees and butterflies, seed for birds in winter
Light pink, mid to late summer	Attract bees and butterflies, seed for birds in winter
Yellow, mid to late summer	Attract bees and butterflies, seed for birds in winter
Deep purple/pink flowers, mid to late summer	Attract bees and butterflies including monarchs, painted ladies, and swallowtails, seed for birds in winter
Yellow flowers, mid to late summer	Attract bees and butterflies, generalist pollinators
Orange-Red, spring	Nectar and pollen for native bees & hummingbirds; cold hardy
Red, late spring - early summer	Nectar and pollen for bees and hummingbirds; cold hardy
Yellow flowers mid summer to fall	Generalist pollinators, bees
Blue daisy-type flowers bloom on deeply cut grey-green foliage in spring	Small generalist pollinators
White, summer	Nectar and pollen for small generalist pollinators- native bees & butterflies
Lavender blue flowers with yellow center, mid summer	Nectar and pollen for small generalist pollinators- native bees & butterflies

Common Name	Latin Name	Height	Width	Exposure
Early Bluetop Fleab.	Erigeron vetensis	10"	8"	Full sun
James' Buckwheat	Eriogonum arcuatum	6' - 12'	6' - 12'	Full sun
Sulfur Buckwheat	Eriogonum umbellatum	10"	12"	Sun/ pt. shade
Wallflower	Erysimum capitatum	24"	24"	Sun/ pt. shade
Rattlesnake master	Eryngium yuccifolium	24"	24"	Full sun
Tulip Gentian	Eustoma grandiflorum	12"	8"	Full sun
Joe Pye Weed	Eutrochium maculatum	48"	36"	Sun/ pt. shade
Blanketflower	Gaillardia aristata	18"	24"	Full sun
Northern Bedstraw	Galium boreale	18"	spreading	Sun/ pt. shade
Scarlet Gaura	Gaura coccinea	8"	Spreading	Full sun
Wild Geranium	Geranium viscosissimum	12"	18"	Full sun
Prairie Smoke	Geum triflorum	12"	12"	Sun/ pt. shade
Broom Snakeweed	Gutierrezia sarothrae	12"	18"	Sun/ pt. shade

Characteristics & notes	Wildlife Value
Blue flowers with yellow center in late spring	Nectar and pollen for small generalist pollinators- native bees & butterflies
Sulphur yellow flowers in late spring and early summer followed persistent flower calyx that is said to resemble buckwheat	Attract bees and generalist pollinators. Eriogonums are "oligolectic" pollinated only by the genus Lycaena (Blue butterflies)
Yellow or orange, early summer	Nectar and pollen for bees and butterflies; biennial
"yucca-like" foliage sends up interesting greenish white flower clusters over a long period. Plant is native to eastern prairies but makes a good companion to native plants	Valuable plant for bees (short and long tonged varieties), wasps, flies, butterflies, skippers, moths, beetles and other plant insects.
Purple cup-shaped flowers in summer, moisture dependent plant of wetland environments	Generalist pollinators
Flowers are large purple umbels, mid to late summer	Attract a large number of bees and butterflies
Yellow, orange and/or red flowers, summer to fall	Nectar and pollen for native bees and butterflies; hairs can cause skin irritation; well-drained soils
Delicate white flowers on lacy dark green foliage, late spring/early summer.	Flowers are mainly pollinated by flies and beetles, but are capable of self-pollination.
Flowers pale pink to pale orange, spring	Possibly pollinated by butterflies and moths
Pink, early, mid summer	Nectar and pollen for small generalist pollinators, specifically butterflies; leaves turn red in fall; well drained soils
Cream to deep pink, spring to early summer	Nectar and pollen for small generalist pollinators, specifically butterflies; moist clay or organic soils
Dark yellow spray of flowers on shrubby plant with deeply cut gray/green foliage, requires no water once established	Nectar and pollen for small generalist pollinators; seeds & cover for birds

Common Name	Latin Name	Height	Width	Exposure
Sneezeweed	Helenium (Dugaldia) hoopesii	24"	24"	Full sun
Annual Sunflower	Helianthus Annuus	72"	48"	
Maximillian's Sunflower	Helianthus maximiliani	60"	48"	Full sun
Nuttals sunflower	Helianthus nutallii	8 - 10 ft.		Full sun
Little Sunflower	Helianthus pumilus	12"-18"	12"-18"	Full sun
Red Yucca	Hesperaloe parviflora	48" - 70"	36"	Full sun
Hairy Golden Aster	Heterotheca villosa	12"	18"	Sun/ pt. shade
Four-Nerve Daisy	Hymenoxys (Tetraneuris) scaposa	6"	12"	Sun/ pt. shade
Bush Morning Glory	Ipomea leptophylla	24"	24"	Sun
Scarlet Gilia	Ipomopsis aggregata	12"	18"	Sun/ pt. shade
Rocky Mountain Iris	Iris Missouriensis	14"	spreading	Full sun
Winterfat	Krascheninnikovia lanata	12"	12"	Full sun
Rocky Mountain Blazing Star	Liatris ligulistylis	36"-48"	12"	Full sun

Characteristics & notes	Wildlife Value
Yellow-orange, late summer	Nectar and pollen for bees and butterflies
Common sunflowers bloom from early summer to frost	Flowers are highly attractive to bees, butterflies, seeds are a favorite food of many song birds, particularly goldfinches
Yellow, late summer - fall	Flowers are highly attractive to bees, butterflies, seeds are a favorite food of many song birds, particularly goldfinches
Yellow, late summer - fall, wetland plant	Flowers are highly attractive to bees, butterflies, seeds are a favorite food of many song birds, particularly goldfinches
small yellow clusters of flowers mid to late summer	Attract small native bees
Pale reddish-orange flowers bloom all summer, plant require no watering even in very dry periods	A particular favorite of hummingbirds
Yellow, summer - fall	Nectar and pollen for small generalist pollinators; specifically butterflies
Yellow - summer	Nectar and pollen for bees and butterflies
Large showy deep pink flowers, mid to late summer	Attractive to pollinators such as butterflies, moths, and long-tongued bees
Red, late summer - fall	Nectar for hummingbirds; well drained soils
Typical blue iris often cover wet montane meadows in early summer, nature combines this with golden banner (thermopsis divaricarpa) with stunning effect	Attracts butterflies including the Melissa blue butterfly
Fluffy white seeds persist from late summer through the winter	Highly nurtitious forage for grazing animals
Pinkish/purple flowers flower stalks late summer	Nectar and pollen for native bees and butterflies; attracts birds

Common Name	Latin Name	Height	Width	Exposure
Gayfeather	Liatris punctata	18"	12"	Full sun
Prairie Blazing star	Liatris pycnostachya	24"-36"	12"	Full sun
Blue Flax	Linum lewisii	18"	6"	Full sun
Cardinal Flower	Lobelia cardinalis	24" - 48"	12" - 24"	Full sun
Great Blue Lobelia	Lobelia siphlitica	24" - 48"	12" - 24"	Full sun
Silver lupine	Lupinus argenteus	24"	12"	Full sun
Bigelow's Tansyaster	Machaeranthera bigelovii	24"	24"	Full sun
Tansy Aster	Machaeranthera tanacetifolia	18"	18"	Full sun
Blackfoot Daisy	Melampodium leucanthum	6"	18"	Sun/ pt. shade
Starflower / Ten Petal Blazing Star	Mentzelia decapetala	18"	18"	Sun
Bractless Starflower / Bractless Blazing Star	Mentzelia nuda	18"	18"	Sun
Yellow Monkey Flower	Mimulus guttatus	12"	spreading	Sun/ pt. shade
Desert Four 'O'clock	Mirabilis multiflora	18"	36"	Full sun
Wild Bergamot/ Bee Balm	Monarda fistulosa	30"	24"	Sun/ pt. shade

Characteristics & notes	Wildlife Value
Pinkish/purple flowers signal the approaching end of summer	Nectar and pollen for native bees and butterflies; attracts birds
Pinkish/purple flowers flower stalks late summer	Nectar and pollen for native bees and butterflies; attracts birds
Blue, late spring - early summer. Re-seeds readily.	Nectar and pollen for small generalist pollinators, specifically native bees and butterflies like the variegated fritillary
Red flowers, summer, wetland plant	Attracts hummingbirds, and butterflies
Blue flowers, summer, wetland plant	Attracts hummingbirds, and butterflies
White to deep purple, mid summer	Nectar and pollen for many pollinators, specifically native bees, hummingbirds, & butterflies- host plant for blue butterfly larva; seeds are toxic if ingested; well drained soils
Deep blue/purple, late summer to fall	Nectar and pollen for small generalist pollinators
Deep blue/purple, mid summer to fall	Nectar and pollen for small generalist pollinators
White, late spring to fall	Nectar and pollen for bees & butterflies; seeds for birds
Spectacular, large white flowers in mid summer, this bienennial with die after flowering and will readily reseed in dry locations	Highly atractive to moths and other nocturnal pollinators
White flowers on bare stems, though a true perennial it is slightly less magnificent than M. decapetala	Highly atractive to moths and other nocturnal pollinators
Clear yellow flowers, spring to mid summer if given sufficient moisture, wetland plant	Exhibits multiple adaptations for pollination by bees
Magenta flowers open in the evening and close by mid day, summer. Tolerates extremely dry conditions	Nectar for evening/nocturnal pollinators- butterflies, hawkmoths, bees, & hummingbirds.
Pink flowers with fragrant foliage, mid summer	Nectar and pollen for native bees/ bumblebees predator wasps, butterflies and hummingbirds, and hawk moths

Common Name	Latin Name	Height	Width	Exposure
Tufted Evening Primrose	Oenothera caespitosa	12"	12"	Full sun
Tall Evening Primrose	Oenothera elata	36"	12"	Full sun
Missouri Evening Primrose	Oenothera macrocarpa	12"	12"	Full sun
Desert Prickly Pear	Opuntia phaeacantha	24"	30"	Full sun
Prickly Pear Cactus	Opuntia polyacantha	12"	24"	Full sun
Showy Locoweed	Oxytropis lambertii	12"	12"	Full sun
White Locoweed	Oxytropis serecia	12"	12"	Full sun
Narrowleaf Beardtongue	Penstemon angustifolius	12"	18"	Full sun
Colorado Beardtongue	Penstemon auriberbis	6"	2"	Full sun
Scarlet Bugler	Penstemon barbatus	48"	12"	Sun/ pt. shade
Mat Penstemon	Penstemon caespitosus	6"	12"	Full sun
Firecracker Penstemon	Penstemon eatonii	24"	18"	Sun/ pt. shade
Lrg. Flowered Beardtongue	Penstemon grandiflorus	36"	18"	Sun/ pt. shade
Palmer's Penstemon	Penstemon palmeri	24"	18"	Full sun
Pineleaf Penstemon	Penstemon pinifolius	12"	18"	Full sun

Characteristics & notes	Wildlife Value
Large, showy white flowers turning pink, spring through summer	Nectar and pollen for bees and butterflies
Yellow flowers on tall stem, mid summer	Nectar and pollen for bees and butterflies
Large yellow flowers in mid summer, in some years European flea beetles completely perforate the foliage of this plant	Nectar and pollen for bees and butterflies
Red/Orange/Yellow, late spring - early summer	food for small mammals; nectar & pollen for insect pollinators- Native bees, moths, & butterflies
Yellow to orange, late spring - early summer	Nectar & pollen for native bees & hummingbirds
Magenta flowers, spring	Nectar and pollen for bees; host for sulfur butterflies; poisonous to livestock. Toxic to humans and livestock
White flowers, spring	Nectar and pollen for bees; host for sulfur butterflies; poisonous to livestock. Toxic to humans and livestock
Blue, late spring - early summer	Nectar and pollen for bumblebees, butterflies and hummingbirds
Violet/lavender, early to mid summer	Nectar and pollen for bees; fruit for birds and other wildlife
Red/pink, extremely long blooming from early summer to late summer	Nectar and pollen for bumblebees, butterflies and hummingbirds
Lavender, early to mid summer	Nectar and pollen for bumblebees, butterflies and hummingbirds
Red, early to mid summer	Nectar and pollen for bumblebees, butterflies and hummingbirds
lavender to blue, early to mid summer	Nectar and pollen for bumblebees, butterflies and hummingbirds
Large showy pink flowers, late spring	Nectar and pollen for bumblebees, butterflies and hummingbirds
Yellow or orange flowers, early to mid summer, "pinemat" foliage	Nectar and pollen for bumblebees, butterflies and hummingbirds

Common Name	Latin Name	Height	Width	Exposure
Desert Beardtongue	Penstemon pseudospectabilis	36"	18"	Sun/ pt. shade
Sidebells Penstemon	Penstemon secundiflorus	20"	12"	Full sun
Rocky Mountain Penstemon	Penstemon strictus	30"	30"	Full sun
Blue Mist Penstemon	Penstemon virens	6"	12"	Sun/ pt. shade
Whipple's Penstemon	Penstemon whippleanus	20"	12"	Sun/ pt. shade
Silky Phacelia	Phacelia sericea	6"	1"	Sun/ pt. shade
Clammyweed	Polanisia dodecandra	12" - 36"	12"	Sun
Jacobs Ladder	Polemonium foliosissimum	12" - 36"	12"	Sun/ pt. shade
Showy Jacob's Ladder	Polemonium pulcherrimum	12"	12"	Sun/ pt. shade
Pasque Flower	Pulsatilla patens	6"	6"	Full sun
Prairie Coneflower	Ratibida columnifera	18"	12"	Full sun
Redspike Coneflower	Ratibida col. umnifera var. pulchra	18"	12"	Full sun
Prairie Coneflower	Ratibida pinnata	24"	18"	Full sun
Black-eyed Susan	Rudbeckia hirta	24"	18"	Full sun

Characteristics & notes	Wildlife Value
Purple/pink, early to mid summer	Nectar and pollen for bumblebees, butterflies and hummingbirds
Lavender, early to mid summer	Nectar and pollen for bumblebees, butterflies and hummingbirds; important forage plants for numerous insects and birds
Blue, Purple, early to mid summer. One of the easiest penstemons to grow	Nectar and pollen for bumblebees, butterflies and hummingbirds; well-drained soils
Light blue to blue/violet, early to mid summer	Nectar and pollen for bumblebees, butterflies and hummingbirds; rock gardens; rocky soils
Wine purple or white, early to mid summer.	Nectar and pollen for bumblebees, butterflies and hummingbirds; sometimes will have ivory flowers
Purple, early summer, late spring early summer	Nectar and pollen for bumblebees, butterflies and hummingbirds
Clusters of small pink and white flowers all summer, annual	Hummingbirds, flies, butterflies
	Bees (particularly bumble bees), flies
Blue, mid summer	Nectar and pollen for bees and butterflies
Lavender, spring to early summer	Nectar and pollen for bees; toxic if ingested
Yellow, mid to late summer	Nectar and pollen for small generalist pollinators- native bees & butterflies
Similar in every way to typical R. Colunifera except flowers are dark reddish-brown	Nectar and pollen for small generalist pollinators- native bees & butterflies
A larger cousin of Ratibida columnifera	Nectar and pollen for small generalist pollinators- native bees & butterflies
Yellow with brown/black center, mid summer	Nectar and pollen for native bees & butterflies; larval host for Gorgone Checkerspot & Bordered Patch butterflies; seeds for birds

Common Name	Latin Name	Height	Width	Exposure
Cutleaf Coneflower / Wild Golden Glow	Rudbeckia lacinata	36" - 48"	24"	Sun/ pt. shade
Brown-eyed Susan	Rudbeckia triloba	36"	24"	Full sun
Pitcher Sage	Salvia azurea var. grandiflora	24"	18"	Sun/ pt. shade
Mojave Sage	Salvia pachyphylla	18"	18"	Full sun
Red Birds in a Tree	Scrophularia macrantha	24"	18"	Sun/ pt. shade
Spearleaf Stonecrop	Sedum lanceolatum	3"	4"	full sun
Broom Groundsel	Senecio spartioides	18"	12"	Full sun
	Sidalcea candida	24" - 36"	12"	Full sun
Pink Checkermallow	Sidalcea neomexicana	24" - 36"	12"	Full sun
Drummond's Catchfly	Silene drummondii	18"	12"	Full sun
Royal Catchfly	Silene regla	18"	12"	Full sun
Prairie Rosinweed	Silphium integrifolium	72"	24"	Full sun
Compass Plant	Silphium laciniatum	60"	24"	Sun/ pt. shade

Characteristics & notes	Wildlife Value
Yellow flowers with greenish yellow center, requires moisture	Nectar and pollen for small generalist pollinators- native bees & butterflies
A native of eastern prairies, similar to black-eyed Susan except taller and branched instead of single stem.	Nectar and pollen for small generalist pollinators- native bees & butterflies
Blue, purple, late summer	Nectar and pollen for native bees & butterflies; attracts hummingbirds
Grey foliage is highly fragrant, flowers are blue and pink, long-lived if it survives initial transplanting, do not water after initial planting!	Attracts hummingbirds
Deep pink to red flowers resemble birds	Highly attractive to hummingbirds
Pale yellow flowers in spring on succulent foliage, this tiny plant often grows in shallow soil that collects on boulders in montane environments	Pollinated by a wide range of bumble bee species
Clear yellow flowers mid to late summer	A large number of insects, including beetles are attracted to this plant which is often the only plant blooming in the hottest part of a dry summer
It is surprising that this elegant white sidalcea is not a more common garden plant. Blooms in mid summer and requires moisture	Nectar and pollen for bees and other pollinators
As showy as it's white flowered cousin, this pink sidalcea also blooms in mid summer and requires moisture	Nectar and pollen for bees and other pollinators
White flowers appear to emerge from a greenish balloon. This mid-summer bloomer requires moisture	Pollinated by bumblebees
This bright red mid-summer bloomer requires moisture	Attracts hummingbirds and butterflies
A deep rooted prairie plant, yellow flowers bloom in mid summer	Attracts butterflies and bees
White flowers bloom in mid summer	Attracts butterflies and bees

Common Name	Latin Name	Height	Width	Exposure
Goldenrod	Solidago canadensis	24"	18"	Full sun
Field Goldenrod	Solidago nemoralis	18"	12"	Full sun
Missouri Goldenrod	Solidago Missouriensis	24"	18"	Full sun
Orange Globemallow	Sphaeralcea munroana	16"	12"	Full sun
Scarlet Globemallow	Sphaeralcea coccinea	6"	spreading	Full sun
Prince's Plume	Stanleya pinnata	30"	24"	Full sun
Drummond's Aster	Symphotrichyum drumondii (Symphyotrichum drummondii)	18"	18"	Full sun
smooth blue aster	Symphyotrichum laeve	18"	18"	Full sun
Porter's Aster	Symphyotrichum porteri	18"	18"	full sun
Golden Banner	Thermopsis divaricarpa	12" - 16"	spreading	Sun/ pt. shade
Western Spiderwort	Tradescantia occidentalis	18"	18"	Sun/ pt. shade
Spiderwort	Tradescantia occidentalis	18"	18"	Sun/part shade

Characteristics & notes	Wildlife Value
Arching yellow flowers in late summer and fall. This plant have mistakenly been linked with hay fever because it blooms that same time as ragweed a common allergen.	As late season flowers goldenrods provide critical forage for bees, butterflies, and other pollinators at time when many species have stopped blooming.
Yellow club shaped flowers bloom mid to late summer.	This plant supports Wavy-lined Emerald (Synchlora aerata) larvae. Field Goldenrod flowers attract butterflies, native bees, honey bees and other pollinators. Songbirds eat the seeds.
Yellow flowers late summer/fall	Attracts numerous bee and butterfly species
Orange flowers, mid summer	Nectar and pollen for small generalist pollinators, specifically native bees
These pale orange flowers are sometimes called "Cowboys Joy" because it is one of the first flowers to bloom on the prairie in spring.	Nectar and pollen for small generalist pollinators, specifically native bees; larval host for fritillary & Small Checkered Skipper butterflies.
Yellow, early to late summer	Nectar for butterflies, native bees, & moths; important forage plants for numerous insects and birds
Blue flowers in mid summer	Attracts bees, butterflies, and caterpillar
Blue flowers in mid summer, grows throughout a wide range from the Rockies to New England	Attracts bees, butterflies, and caterpillar
White flowers in mid summer	Attracts bees, butterflies, and caterpillar
Yellow bloom mid to late spring, can spread aggressively, toxic if ingested	Pollinated by bumblebees
Blue flowers on fleshy blue-green stems	Benefits native bees
Purple, late spring to early summer	Nectar and pollen for native bees and butterflies

Common Name	Latin Name	Height	Width	Exposure
Prairie Verbena	Verbena bipinnatifida / Glandularia bipinnatifida	6"	12"	Full sun
Blue Vervain	Verbena hastata	48"	12"	Sun/pt. shade
Hoary Vervain	Verbena stricta	24"	18"	Full sun
Showy Goldeneye	Viguiera multiflora	24"	18"	Full sun
Prairie Zinnia	Zinnia grandiflora	6"	12"	Full sun

Characteristics & notes	Wildlife Value
Purple flowers, early summer to late summer	Nectar and pollen for bees and butterflies, attracts birds, short-lived perennial
Purple flowers, mid summer to late summer, requires moisture	Nectar for pollinators
Purple flowers, mid summer to late summer, tolerates dry sites	Nectar for pollinators
Yellow flowers, summer, tolerates dry sites	Attracts birds & butterflies, reseeds aggressively
Golden yellow, mid to late summer	Nectar and pollen for native bees, butterflies, & moths

CHAPTER 16

SUSTAINABLE LANDSCAPING

The Crisis of Turfgrass

Between 1900 and 2021, the United States population more than quadrupled, from 76.2 million to 327.2 million. Over the same period, Americans moved in huge numbers from rural settings to suburbs and cities. As a result, urban and suburban landscapes expanded exponentially and cover significant portions of the land. In *Bringing Nature Home*, a groundbreaking book focused on the impacts to wildlife due to habitats being replaced by landscaping, Douglas Tallamy presents the following statistics:

- Ninety-eight percent of the Lower Forty-eight states has been altered for human use.
- Almost forty-two million acres in the US are covered by pavement.
- Turfgrass covers more than forty million acres, and more herbicide and pesticide are used on turfgrass (per square foot) than any other crop.
- Eight-hundred-million gallons of gas are used to mow American lawns every year.

Although our growing population and a changing climate will reduce available water, thus far, we have made virtually no effort to conserve water in landscaping. The rampant use of irrigated turfgrass in the American West presents a critical yet seldom-mentioned ecological crisis. It represents not only a lack of awareness of the region in which we live but a profound lack of imagination as well, since we are fortunate to have so many beautiful and well-adapted native plants that can be used in landscaping.

Because the human footprint has become so extensive, and typical ornamental landscapes filled with exotic plant species offer little or no benefit for wildlife, we need to rethink the purpose of landscape design. Fortunately, a growing number of homeowners, developers, and landscape designers are becoming aware that our gardens can, and must, be much more than simply pretty. Well-designed native landscapes can help create connectivity through our growing urban and suburban corridor and benefit wildlife in the places where we live.

Habitat Garden Maintenance

After we have designed and installed a suitable landscape for our Western climate, utilizing native plants and taking advantage of the site's unique attributes, it's essential that our garden management practices align with the goals of creating and supporting wildlife habitat. However, the practices of many landscape management companies are directly counter to the goals of gardening for wildlife.

One of the unique and wonderful things about gardening in the West is the way that landscapes persist in winter, like dried floral arrangements that last until spring. Looking out on the winter landscape, the faded colors of dried grasses and snowcaps on dried flowers are beautiful in their own right and remind us of the summer garden.

This natural gardening style provides four-season interest, but there are other important reasons not to cut back plants until spring. The bright winter sunshine in the Rocky Mountain West can cause the ground to freeze and thaw repeatedly. This continual freezing and thawing can be hard on plants. Leaving the previous season's growth to shade the

After frost

ground can minimize this while retaining moisture at the roots.

Beneficial insects may be hibernating in the hollow stems of plants in our winter garden. By removing old growth too early, we can unknowingly be removing beneficial pollinators. Winter can be a difficult time for birds, and they can often be seen picking through leaves, seeking insects on a warm winter day, picking the last few seeds from dried flower heads, and nibbling persistent fruits softened by the frost.

It's common for landscape management companies to prune shrubs excessively and cut back ornamental grasses and perennials in the fall instead of spring. From an aesthetic perspective, plants are typically more attractive when allowed to have their natural form. The practice of shearing every shrub into a green meatball has fortunately gone out of fashion in many places. The goal of low-maintenance natural landscape design is to choose the right plants in the first place, those that fit the space at their mature size.

Excessive shearing can be stressful for plants. It can interrupt flowering and fruiting cycles, and prevent shrubs from being utilized for nesting by birds. A good practice for reducing shrub size is regenerative

Spring

Summer

Fall

Winter

pruning, which is done in wintertime, cutting plants back by up to two-thirds of their height. This is not a practice that should be repeated every year on most shrubs.

It's also important to know whether shrubs bloom on new wood or old wood. Plants that bloom on old wood include American plum and golden currant. The time to prune these plants is immediately after flowering, before new buds set. Pruning at other times will be essentially removing the next year's flowers. Woods' rose and potentilla are examples of shrubs that bloom on new wood and can be pruned in spring.

Pesticides, organic or otherwise, are virtually never needed in native plant landscapes. Certain pesticides can have devastating consequences on pollinators. Neonicotinoids, which are systemic insecticides that may be applied by growers that produce nursery plants, can persist in soil for more than 1,000 days. These insecticides will kill insects that come into contact with them, including beneficial pollinators that we may be trying to attract to our gardens. It's extremely important to know where our plants are grown and if insecticides have been applied to them.

Insects like aphids are generally not an ongoing problem. If they become unsightly, they can simply be washed off with a hose. Typically, aphids only persist when the weather is around 70°F. In the hot and dry summer season, they usually subside.

Fallen leaves are often removed in traditional landscape maintenance, but this is not necessary in native landscapes. A cover of leaves can help plants and wildlife survive the winter, and after decomposing, they return nutrients to the soil.

SECTION III

A CULTURE OF ENVIRONMENTAL STEWARDSHIP

Bird watchers at High Plains Environmental Center

CHAPTER 17

ENGAGING COMMUNITY

The biggest challenge in the transition toward a more sustainable landscaping style is actually a social issue rather than a horticultural one. It's essential that all parties understand the timelines involved in establishing areas of native vegetation, how it will look at various phases of establishment, how it will be maintained, and why native landscapes are essential. You might think that in a neighborhood marketed as "Nature in your Backyard," people would understand that native grass is not being mowed for a reason, but that is not always the case.

Outreach needs to be intentional and ongoing to establish and maintain a peaceful coexistence with nature. Signage, classes, newsletters, flyers, and videos are among the strategies we use. It's also important to have community buy-in to promote an understanding of the behaviors necessary to protect wildlife, as well as people and pets, in the habitat that has been created.

We have seen natural areas as well as wildlife abused, sometimes cruelly but usually inadvertently, out of a lack of awareness of the consequences of things like creating social trails through habitat areas or allowing pets off-leash. When Front Range Community College conducted a BioBlitz in 2019, counting birds, fish, mammals, and other wildlife on HPEC property, their wildlife cameras picked up dogs off-leash one after another. The report pointed out that wildlife habitat would be severely impacted if dogs continued to wander off leash.

Following that, HPEC hired a private security company to patrol the trails on bicycles. The public responds differently to a uniformed officer, and we prefer to focus the energies of our staff on stewardship and education. Both education and enforcement are necessary strategies for protecting open space.

Neighborhood Open Space Guidelines

HPEC is closely integrated with the Lakes at Centerra neighborhood where we are located and manage the community's open space. Because many of the houses in our neighborhood have walkout basements with a significant slope from the front to the back of the house, contractors sometimes want to go through the open space to reach the backs of houses. However, any disturbance in open space can knock down vegetation and create ruts where water collects, and weeds begin to establish. Any kind of disturbance is counter to the goals of establishing native open space (relatively) free of weeds. We have found it helpful to mark all entrances to the open space with signs that say vehicles are prohibited. At times it has been necessary to require contractors to pay for damages to open space, but recovery to native grass is a slow process and prevention is by far preferable.

Sometimes residents throw grass clippings, branches, or potting soil over their back fence, regarding these materials as "natural." Although these materials will eventually break down, they can smother native vegetation in the process, and branches can obstruct the mowing done as a courtesy to keep vegetation away from their fence line. Garden waste must not be allowed to accumulate in open natural areas.

We have also seen homeowners mowing or spraying areas with herbicide outside of their lots. As we've discussed in the previous chapters, mowing has specific purposes in managing natural areas. Still it can stress grasses and facilitate the growth of weeds if done excessively or at the wrong time. Herbicide applications by qualified natural area professionals are usually at lower dilution rates and on

The natural drainage and storm water detention areas in Centerra take time and specialized care to grow in and mature. That's why we have the High Plains Environmental Center (HPEC) actively manage them throughout the community. The HPEC takes newly constructed areas from raw dirt and turns them into wonderful habitats.

THE LAKES
AT CENTERRA

At time of planting

After a couple of growing seasons

What can you do to help?

Don't dispose of yard waste or grass clippings from your home into the natural area.

Leave the weed management in the natural area to the professionals.

DO stay on the trails and sidewalks when out walking or biking.

DO keep your pets on a leash and pick up after them.

Live and let live – please don't disturb or harass wildlife.

Signage

specific targets than those applied by home gardeners. EPA restrictions on herbicides that can be used in or adjacent to wetlands are in place to protect aquatic animals.

Some people place dispensers containing rodenticide outside their houses. We have even found them in the community open space! Native grasses and shrubs will attract rodents. Mice and voles will be able to find cover, as well as seeds, in unmown native grass. However, that is the basis of habitat. Hawks, owls, eagles, snakes, foxes, and coyotes all include rodents in their diet. Because predators are at the top of the food chain, they are vulnerable. Many do not survive past their second year due to starvation. Raptors, including hawks and owls, or any other predators (including cats and dogs), that ingest poisoned rodents can be exposed to secondary poisoning.

Storm drains in many neighborhoods, including ours, flow directly into drainages, ponds, and lakes. Phosphates from soap used to wash cars in a driveway or the over-application of fertilizer can contribute to nutrient runoff that can kill fish.

Redtail hawk

Great horned owl

No doubt some people in the neighborhood, if asked what they thought of the High Plains Environmental Center, would say, "High Plains what?" Neighborhoods are more transient than they have been in previous times. The typical home resells every ten years, and many people move more often than that. It's not possible to engage every single individual. Still, many people, when asked about why they moved to the neighborhood, report it was because of us, because of the birds, trails, open space, and nature surrounding them. Developers are becoming increasingly aware that access to nature, trails, and open space are major marketing points for neighborhoods and home sales. Real estate statistics support the fact that homes near natural areas are more valuable. Our job is to facilitate the peaceful coexistence of the two.

To help the developer in our neighborhood accomplish their restoration and stewardship roles, HPEC participates as an advisor on the Centerra Design Review Committee. We have the ability and responsibility to veto seed mixes that contain inappropriate species or landscape plants that can potentially become invasive. HPEC often functions as project manager for restoration projects within Centerra, providing input on suitable plant material, landscape design, and restoration protocols.

HPEC offers public lectures on environmental stewardship and sustainable living throughout the year and community events such as a fall pumpkin festival, nature scavenger hunts, bird walks, and native plant sales. For more than a decade, we have maintained a close partnership with the Thompson School District in Loveland and hosted numerous school field trips. HPEC has also provided material support and guidance for horticultural projects at individual schools and offers an internship program intended to lead to career development in biology, horticulture, agriculture, and related sciences. HPEC provides consultation and restoration services for projects up and down the Front Range and has offered presentations focused on landscaping with native plants and restoring natural areas, as far away as the Rhode Island School of Design and Harvard University.

Since 2005, HPEC has cohosted an annual Landscaping with Colorado Native Plants Conference in collaboration with partner organizations: including the Butterfly Pavilion, CSU Department of Horticulture

Drainages in neighborhood open space

and Landscape Architecture, CSU Extension, Colorado Native Plant Master Program, Colorado Native Plant Society, Denver Botanic Gardens, and Front Range Wild Ones, and author Susan J Tweit. The conference focuses on various aspects of landscaping with native plants presented in two tracks, one for novices and one for experienced native plant gardeners.

We have a particular interest in nature programs for children. Like the masters of any craft, we are particularly interested in meeting young people with the inclination and talent for the work we do. We feel we are charged with inspiring the land stewards of the next generation. Given the opportunity to connect with wild beings in their formative years, young people have the potential to become advocates for conservation in their adulthood. Like many others who work in environmental education, we feel the weight of making every effort to ensure we

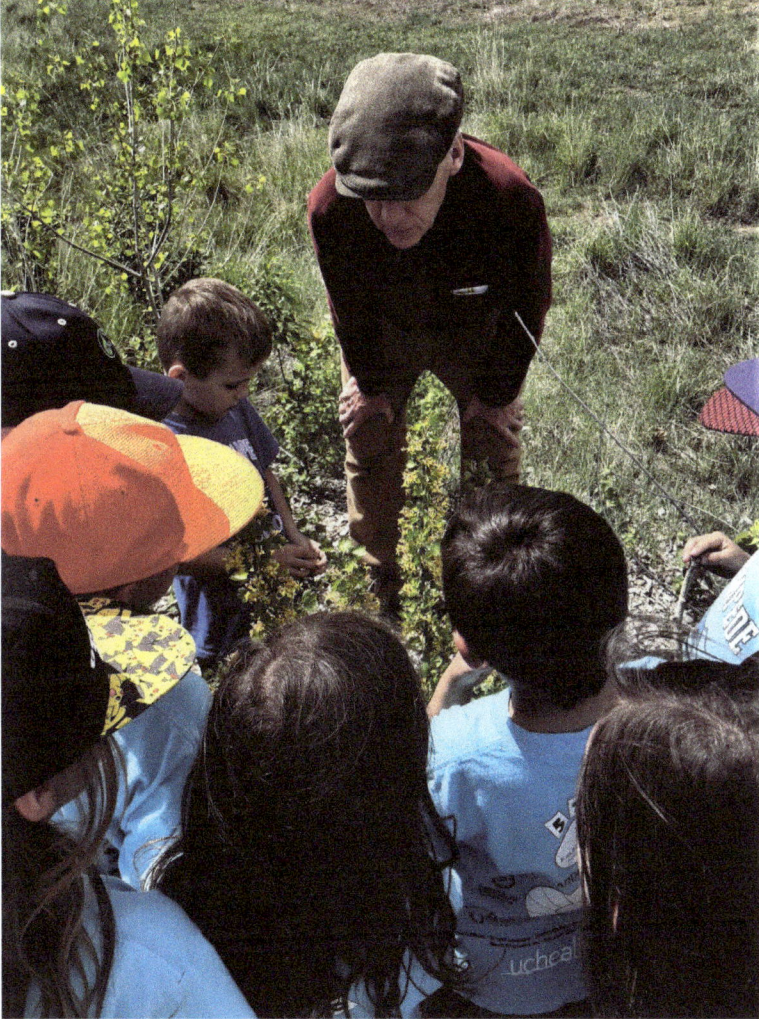

Nature programs for children can inspire the land stewards of the next generation.

are not just leading children to develop a love for nature, only to have them realize how much has been lost later in their lives. Nature is dynamic, nature is creative, nature is opportunistic. By providing a little care, attention, and awareness, we can make a tremendous difference for wildlife.

CHAPTER 18

WORKING WITH VOLUNTEERS

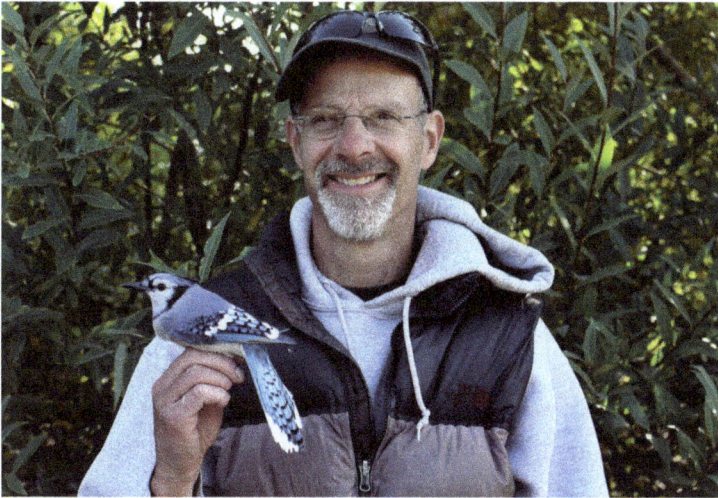

Scott Rashid, director of Colorado Avian Research and Rehabilitation Institute (CARRI)

Programs: Citizen Science Bird Banding

High Plains Environmental Center has partnered with the Colorado Avian Research and Rehabilitation Institute (CARRI) on citizen science projects to band birds for research purposes. Banding helps to identify migration patterns, lifespans, and populations of bird species. For participants of all ages, holding tiny birds that have been gently extracted from mist-nets may be the only time in their lives that they come this close to these creatures.

Scott Rashid, the director of CARRI, has an amazing rapport with these birds. Scott has a knack for reading participants' energy, instructing them to relax, and then saying, "You're not relaxed," when observing the bird's reactions. Birds always appear relaxed when Scott holds them. He shows participants how to stroke the beak of our barn owls, which simulates the way owls preen each other, and it always calms them.

The height of our collaboration is a live-streaming owl nest camera where we can observe what barn owls are doing without disturbing them. A group of volunteers installed a nesting box in 2007 in the rafters of the barn. Barn owl pairs have occupied the barn since the spring of 2008. A camera was added to the nesting box in 2012. The owl cam, hosted on the CARRI website, has been watched by thousands of people from as far away as Australia. Since there was no electric power at the barn, HPEC staff built a solar-powered system to drive the owl cam.

The American kestrel is a tiny falcon that feeds on insects, mice, and small birds. A kestrel box with a nest cam is mounted on top of the HPEC classroom. The kestrel cam is also hosted on the CARRI site. The kestrels produce one brood a year, and the owls sometimes produce two broods based on food availability. The young birds are banded before they leave the nest box so we can learn where they go. These banding events are always a very special opportunity to view these amazing birds up close.

Virtually everything at HPEC, except for our building, was built or planted by volunteers. Working with volunteers is a unique situation. Volunteers are neither employees nor program participants. A successful volunteer project has just the right amount of instruction and transmission of an organization's vision and goals, combined with accomplishing a task. If there is too much focus on the task, the project becomes like a work camp. Participants may leave without learning much about the place where they have been. If there is too much focus on creating an enjoyable and educational experience for volunteers, the task may not be accomplished, and an opportunity will be lost.

A good volunteer project begins with a thorough explanation of how to complete the task and why it is important. The work should be explained very carefully so that it can be done correctly. It's also

Barn Owl

Baby kestrels

important to set time parameters such as "This project will be from 9:00 to 12:00," with an expectation that volunteers will commit to the project's completion.

There can sometimes be a tendency for individuals overseeing volunteers to get wrapped up in doing the work themselves. This is a mistake because volunteers require supervision. With many people working on a project at the same time, things can go off the rails quickly; picture the scene in the *Sorcerer's Apprentice*, from Walt Disney's *Fantasia*, where dozens of broomsticks are carrying buckets of water and flooding the castle. When not adequately supervised, volunteers can injure themselves, damage the land, or make errors that can result in the death of plants or damage to materials. Volunteer project leaders primarily serve to advise and support volunteers.

Most importantly, the contribution of volunteers must be acknowledged, and volunteers should be thanked repeatedly. Sometimes offering snacks or small tokens of appreciation is helpful.

At HPEC, volunteering is one of our strongest outreach programs. The contribution that volunteers make is unlike monetary donations. Volunteers contribute their time and become personally invested in the natural area, gardens, or other projects they work on. They form a bond with the host organization and their fellow volunteers.

Sometimes volunteers arrive as a fully formed group with their own leaders, whether coworkers at a business, schoolmates, or members of the same church or club. For these organizations, volunteering can deepen relationships and help the group to function better as a team. It is much easier to work with volunteers already formed into a group than create a group out of individuals who have just met.

It's essential to match the abilities of volunteers to a particular task. We sometimes design a volunteer day based on prior knowledge of the volunteers' ages, physical strength, and other qualifications. For volunteer projects to be successful, they need to be extremely well-planned with all the project stages, and what materials, tools, and other elements will be required carefully thought through.

Overseeing, answering questions, and providing instruction to dozens of people at one time can be exhausting and unproductive. It's critical to have a high enough ratio of project leaders to volunteers.

Volunteers for Outdoor Colorado planting native shrubs & trees

Although this is an unpleasant topic, the reality or even the insinuation of sexual misconduct is a concern that any volunteer organization must take seriously. For this reason, we follow the "two-deep leadership" model used by the Boy Scouts, where there are always two adults working together with minors.

When all of these elements come together, projects can be accomplished in a matter of hours that might otherwise have taken paid staff weeks to do. In the process, individuals can form a bond with the organization and the landscape that may persist for years. We have seen volunteers return to HPEC and point out with a sense of pride, accomplishment, and belonging, the trees and gardens they planted.

We have engaged volunteers in planting wetland plants, grasses, wildflowers, shrubs, and trees. Our volunteers have installed signs and built kiosks, greenhouses, raised garden beds, and a shade arbor. Volunteers have helped enhance habitat for specific species by creating bee hotels, bat boxes, owl and kestrel nesting boxes, birdhouses, and

Bee Hotel

an osprey nesting platform. Our staff does very little that volunteers cannot do if given sufficient instruction, oversight, and support.

Citizen science is a place where volunteering and public education come together in equal measure. This is a way of involving people in monitoring wildlife, including banding birds, counting frogs and toads based on their mating calls, or counting pollinators through observation. With a little bit of training, citizen scientists can help study species by contributing their data to websites such as iNaturalist.org and eBird. org. Citizen scientists can also help count and monitor plants by laying out transects, evenly spaced lines of string, that help estimate the numbers of a particular plant species on a site.

Putting up osprey platform (Photo: HPEC archive)

Ospreys have occupied our nesting platform every year since 2007.

CHAPTER 19

LIVING WITH WILDLIFE: A SUBURBAN NATURALIST JOURNAL

Owlets in their nest on top of Pier One sign

H abitat opportunities created in urban and suburban open space, stormwater ponds, and green roofs are part of what is known as novel ecosystems. Unlike large, intact ecosystems, novel ecosystems may present opportunities for specific species that may not have existed before in this particular arrangement. One great example of this is the peregrine falcon habitat in large cities, where the falcons nest on high buildings similar to the cliffs in their natural habitat. The falcons thrive by hunting pigeons, which are abundant in the city.

Green roofs are rooftops vegetated with plants that help reduce the urban heat island effect and slow and filter stormwater runoff. Ground-nesting birds such as the killdeer, whose young and eggs are typically vulnerable to predators, have discovered these predator-free zones provided by green roofs and benefited from them. Novel ecosystems do not replace large intact natural areas. Still, they help create connectivity through the urban corridor and allow people to observe and interact with wildlife daily.

Some of the species that can benefit the most from the *Suburbitat* model are insect pollinators. The global plight of the honeybee, a non-native insect that is critically important for agriculture, has become widely known in the last decade. However, vast numbers of native pollinators, bees, butterflies, and other insects have experienced a similar decline. This is largely due to the destruction of native plants on which they depend and collateral (or intentional) damage from insecticides. Because these animals have extremely short lifespans, their numbers can increase significantly in a short amount of time after the reintroduction of native plants.

At HPEC, we are endlessly fascinated by observing many kinds of pollinators in our gardens and the specific associations that can be observed between particular plants and pollinators. Even some wasps can be important pollinators and may help to control other insects. However, the European paper wasp is highly destructive to our native butterfly population and should be discouraged. Paper wasp nests resemble honeycomb and are found under eaves of buildings, in garden sheds, even in outdoor barbecues. Nests made by founding queens in springtime are the most easily destroyed. Later in the season, this is perhaps the one case where we might argue that an insecticide should be used. Please note that these should not be confused with the paper sacs that bald-faced hornets, which are harmless if left alone, make in trees and shrubs.

Outdoor porch lights can be harmful to moths and other nocturnal insects. Lights can confuse the insects and can and cause their deaths. Consider installing motion-activated lights instead.

Colorado is home to three different cottontail rabbit species: the mountain cottontail, the desert cottontail, and the eastern cottontail.

Bigelow's tansy aster (*Machaeranthera bigelovii*) and orange sulphur butterfly

The eastern cottontail, found in Front Range communities, thrives in developed areas and has dramatically increased in our region in recent years. This is in part because they follow a natural cycle where they will increase to their maximum capacity and then die off from diseases such as Tularemia. It is inadvisable to touch a dead rabbit (or any animal found dead) for this reason.

Recent growth of the rabbit population may be connected with a cyclical decline of red foxes. A decade or so ago, foxes were common along the Front Range. Since then, red foxes seem to have died off in large numbers due at least in part to mange caused by a parasitic mite that some domestic dogs also carry.

Dogs can also carry other parasites and pathogens that may "spill over" into wildlife, as well as humans. This is why signs are often posted in natural areas that say, "Dog waste spreads disease."

Human beings often see problems with wildlife but don't see how we have contributed to or even created the problem. Coexisting with wildlife is a matter of understanding how our actions influence nature, and fine-tuning the suburbitat.

Eastern cottontail

The American bald eagle represents a spectacular story of species recovery. Eagles breed in mountain areas and unpopulated river corridors but have become relatively common along the wintertime Front Range. Young bald eagles are brown, flecked with white on their undersides, and don't get a characteristic white head and tail until they are five years old. However, young bald eagles can be identified by their tell-tale orange legs. Though the bald eagle's primary food is fish, they eat geese and ducks in winter when water is frozen over. Eagles typically pick off lame waterfowl, but they are quite capable of breaking a bird's bones with their powerful feet.

Canada geese are another species that are commonly found in Front Range communities. At one time, there was an intentional effort on the part of Colorado Parks and Wildlife to establish year-round populations of Canada geese in Fort Collins. They might have overshot the goal a little bit on this one, as the geese have become extremely prolific. Nonetheless, watching the fly-in of Canada geese to lakes and ponds in Northern Colorado can be an amazing wildlife experience.

American bald eagle

Turfgrass is one of the geese's favorite foods. Out of fear of predators, geese tend to avoid a shoreline that is heavily vegetated with shrubs. Ponds where grass has been mowed right up to the water's edge create a haven for geese. If geese become a problem, consider altering the landscape to make it a less conducive habitat for them.

Although many people consider it fun and even a generous act to feed geese and ducks, it's actually harmful to them. Feeding waterfowl can cause overcrowding, which can aid in the spread of avian diseases and contribute to algae blooms in lakes that can kill fish and other aquatic life. The spread of parasites that cause "swimmer's itch" is another byproduct of overcrowding.

Feeding processed foods that contain high amounts of starch and sugar to geese and ducks can cause malnutrition and make them unable to fly. Waterfowl are better off when they are required to hunt for highly nutritious natural foods such as mollusks and aquatic plants.

Geese can become aggressive during the breeding season and will defend their nest or young from predators. It is best to give them their space during these times. Occasionally other species, such as snow geese, will join with Canada geese when they've been separated from their flock.

At HPEC, we have debated whether it's a good idea to feed birds or not. On the one hand, feeding concentrates birds, making them more vulnerable to predators and possibly facilitating the spread of avian diseases. However, a well-placed and properly maintained feeder can allow wildlife enthusiasts an opportunity to view birds that they may not be able to see otherwise.

We much prefer the idea of planting the plants that the birds depend on for habitat, food, and shelter. We have planted large numbers of native shrubs to increase cover and forage for birds, and it's our policy to encourage sunflowers for songbirds in our gardens and open space.

All this said, with so much habitat loss and pressures on birds due to climate change, feeding birds can be beneficial if it's done properly. More than feeding, the availability of water in wintertime can be extremely important for birds. Colorado winters are dry, and when water is frozen for long periods, birds can become parched. A small backyard pond or birdbath with a stock tank heater can attract a remarkable number of birds.

Baby birds are often found on the ground in spring. Usually, the bird's parents are nearby out of sight, attending the baby. The best thing to do is to simply leave them alone. Birds are often hit by cars or smash into windows. Sometimes the window strikes are unintentional. Birds are only seeing a reflection and don't realize the glass is solid. Other times, particularly during the breeding season, birds may fly at their reflection, thinking they are chasing away competing members of their species.

Snow goose

White pelicans have changed migration patterns to capitalize on manmade ponds and inundated gravel pits along the Front Range.

Cedar waxwings often appear in midwinter gorging on persistent fruit softened by the frost.

Sometimes these injured birds can recover by being kept warm and allowed to rest for a while. It's very important to create a little nest for them. A twisted and coiled section of newspaper works well for this. The nest helps to hold the birds upright, keeping the air sacs in their sides from collapsing and leading to suffocation. The nest can be placed in a box in a quiet place. The ability of the bird to recover will be dependent on the extent of their injuries. If they do recover and become active, they should be released immediately.

The great blue heron is one of the largest birds in North America. They can grow up to four-and-a-half feet tall with a wingspan of over six feet in length. Many Native American tribes considered this to be a sacred bird because of its high degree of adaptability. It gracefully wades in the water and is beautiful in flight, but it nests in trees, somewhat awkwardly, in large rookeries.

Blue herons are frequent visitors to natural areas that contain water but require a setback of over 600 feet from any trail for breeding areas. These birds can be seen wading, sometimes remaining motionless for long periods, waiting for fish. When the heron does make a catch, it

Heron rookery

Blue heron

Turkey

will flip the fish so that it will go down their throat headfirst. If the heron does not swallow that fish headfirst, the bird can choke to death. Blue herons are formidable hunters that can eat mice and small birds as well.

Over the last several decades, wild turkey populations have increased significantly. Wild turkeys are extremely intelligent and highly adaptable. Turkeys will forage for seed underneath bird feeders adjacent to wild areas and glean grains, especially corn, out of farm fields.

The Anasazi, ancient Pueblo farmers of the Southwest who grew corn, partially domesticated wild turkeys. Feeding wild turkeys is not recommended because it artificially increases their numbers.

Raccoons are common in suburban areas. If you find baby raccoons, they have often been left in place by their mother, who will return for them. If the mother does not return, a wildlife agency should be notified. Raccoons are clever and playful, but they can be dangerous when approached by people and pets. Keeping pet food and trash secured and out of sight can keep these animals from becoming a nuisance.

Raccoon

Mink

Mink are relatively common in Colorado, particularly near riparian areas. Like all members of the weasel family, mink are formidable hunters, and rodents are their favorite foods.

Turtles need to sun themselves to store vitamin D to help form their hard shell. Habitat for turtles can be improved by anchoring logs in place for this purpose. It also allows visitors to the natural area an opportunity for viewing them.

CHAPTER 20

WILDLIFE/HUMAN CONFLICTS

Coyotes are highly successful species and have adapted to man-made alterations from Massachusetts to California. One of the reasons for the coyote's success is the plasticity of the species, which causes females to produce larger litters if their population is declining. Killing or removing coyotes from an area will cause an increase in reproduction.

Coyotes are also highly adaptable. At HPEC, where we have very few upland areas where coyotes typically den, they choose areas where cattails provide thick cover instead. Coyotes help control mice, voles, and rabbits, but they are capable of killing cats and small dogs. Unless a coyote is rabid, it's highly unlikely that they would harm a person, but they are powerful wild animals and should be treated with caution. People who are concerned about coyotes should not walk alone between dusk and dawn. Pets, of course, should never be allowed to wander freely in natural areas.

Before leaving the topic of large predators, bears and mountain lions do not typically live in suburban developments. Still, they are not infrequent visitors to neighborhoods in the Rocky Mountain West. A mountain lion with a tracking collar left Rocky Mountain National Park, headed east across Colorado into Nebraska, went south across Kansas into Oklahoma, and crossed New Mexico to return to Colorado, all in less than a year.

Wildlife cameras in natural areas along the Front Range frequently show large animals such as elk, bighorn sheep, bears, and lions. Hikers approach, and animals move off; hikers leave, and animals return. Many hunters and photographers are aware that the best way to see animals is to sit quietly and wait.

The general wisdom for encountering a mountain lion is to avoid eye contact, make yourself look large, and back away slowly. Others say to move sideways to avoid tripping. The National Park Service says to stand your ground if a bear charges you (good luck with that).

Snakes can provoke strong emotional reactions in people, but they can also be extremely beneficial because many feed primarily on rodents. We have never seen a rattlesnake in Centerra, but we do have many large bull snakes, western garter snakes, and occasionally green racers.

A story was related to us about a young woman who became extremely upset about a bull snake sunning by the swimming pool in our neighborhood. The girl's grandfather killed the snake, and other community members were upset about it and said, "This is an area for wildlife!" We consider this an extremely good sign when our neighbors become the ambassadors of the *Suburbitat* mission.

In the 1800s, beaver pelts were used to make hats that were the height of fashion in Europe. Beaver trapping was the main occupation of mountain men who were among the first white people to enter the Rocky Mountain West. As a result of extensive trapping, the beaver came close to extinction, which in turn had a profound impact on other species that benefited from the beaver's damming of waterways and wetland habitat creation. Landowners who have beavers on their property may be concerned about water rights issues associated with the evaporative loss from ponds that beavers build. McGregor Ranch in Estes Park, Colorado, found some creative ways of working with this.

MacGregor Ranch is a 1.8 square mile working ranch and museum in Estes Park, Colorado. The ranch has implemented some progressive land management strategies, including the reintroduction of beavers to the property. Beaver dams can slow water down enough to allow pastures to be subirrigated, saturated from below ground. Subirrigated fields and pastures may not need supplemental irrigation even in dry

Black bear

Beaver

periods. However, beaver activity can cause problems for landowners who, by law, cannot restrict the flow of waterways.

Wildlife biologists have long argued that a beaver dam does not stop the flow of a river. The water still passes through at a slower release rate, providing numerous ecological benefits along the way. Beavers are viewed as stealing the water, and even municipalities are required to remove them.

MacGregor Ranch enlisted the CSU Wildlife Society's help to build a "beaver deceiver" that allows water to flow through the pond at its historical volume. They mapped the entire site with GIS. They measured the pond depth and calculated the water flow. The beaver deceiver was not an entirely new idea, but the mathematical calculation that the group added to the concept was unique.

The result was a twenty-foot-long PVC pipe, perforated at the top, with a good cap on it so it didn't create a vortex, which would cause the beaver to want to plug it. The water passed through the pipe at a 40-degree angle through the dam face, all of which was part of the calculation. They calculated the historic water flow and installed a ball valve at the bottom of the pipe to regulate the amount of water that was being released. Beavers were wiped out twice by floods, but they have returned to the site.

In another beaver project at a Fort Collins natural area along the Poudre River, volunteers painted a slurry of sand and concrete onto the base of trees to protect them from gnawing beavers. The treatment has worked well and lasted for decades. Undesirable tree species were not treated, leaving the beavers plenty to chew on.

The black-tailed prairie dog is an inhabitant of the shortgrass prairie, reduced to less than 3 percent of its former range. Aside from loss of habitat and poisoning by landowners, sylvatic plague, an introduced pathogen, has had devastating impacts on prairie dogs and other North American mammals. Yet this animal that, by the typical criteria of 97 percent habitat loss, would be listed as an endangered species, is instead listed as a "noxious rodent pest" in Colorado. Tourists marvel and delight at prairie dog towns in our national parks. Yet the same animals are eradicated from urban sites to make way for development or simply removed as a "nuisance population."

Beaver tree paint

Prairie dog family

A prairie dog colony's typical pattern is to expand, leaving behind an overgrazed site and moving on to better prospects. This is not possible in urban environments. Prairie dogs will often strip native vegetation off a site when they become landlocked. The site then becomes weedy and ecologically degraded, ruining habitat potential for birds, pollinators, and other wildlife. Not infrequently, the prairie dog population will crash due to malnutrition and disease.

Prairie dogs living in the shortgrass prairie are considered a keystone species on which many other species depend. However, although prairie dogs can provide a food source for hawks, most wildlife biologists say that urban prairie dogs have little ecological value except for educational value.

Urban prairie dogs remind us of the shortgrass prairie that previously existed where our cities now rise. They provide a sense of place and a connection with the primordial past. They're educational, and they're fun to watch, but they need to be managed. People line up on either side of this issue with a range of positions from "the only good prairie dog is a dead prairie dog" to "never harm any animals." For urban prairie dogs to be sustainable, their population size needs to be maintained at a level proportionate to the sites carrying capacity. In short, a portion of the prairie dog population must be periodically removed from the site or killed. Removal involves trapping the animals and taking them to another location. One of the complications of removal is the danger of communicating diseases to populations in the new location. In some cases, prairie dogs removed from the site are fed to other wild animals at breeding and rehabilitation facilities.

The lethal option is not pleasant. In the best case, it involves poisoning the animals with a product that turns into a gas when ingested. Because the product is short-lived, there is little potential for collateral damage to other species. Conversely, the use of anticoagulant rodenticides can be disastrous because of their potential for secondary poisoning of other species.

For the sake of not romanticizing the lives of animals, and having a sort of Walt Disney outlook, it's worthwhile to note the prairie dogs will eat their pups if the population becomes too confined. Our best service to animals lies within our ability to see them as they truly are, not as beings like ourselves, but rather as beings of value in their own right.

Not assuming responsibility for landlocked prairie dog populations in urban environments is a dereliction of duty. To not see prairie dogs as beings that can feel pain and have the same will to live and remain free as any other creature is an empathic failure. This issue will remain with us until someone invents contraceptives for prairie dogs or we begin to design cities with greater permeability for our wildlife.

Owl Epilogue

We had a terrible experience in the fall of 2020 when we went up into the loft of our barn and found our entire family of barn owls, animals that we watched hatch from eggs, dead from rodent poisoning. These birds died from an anticoagulant type of rodenticide. Our beautiful birds bled to death from every orifice in their bodies. It was a horrible scene and a devastating gut punch to everyone involved with HPEC.

Working to protect wildlife can be fraught with heartbreak and frustration. At times it feels like one step forward and two steps back, but it is important and necessary work. We are planning to add light-weight tracking devices when we band our owls next year so we will be able to see where they go and where these poisons are being used.

Placing mouse bait poisons outdoors is unnecessary and danger-ous. A safer strategy is to prevent mice from entering your home by sealing any exterior cracks or opening around pipes, etc. If you have rodents, indoors snap traps work quickly and effectively. If you decide to use a rodenticide choose a type that is sealed and does not allow the rodent to escape after ingesting poison.

Poisoned barn owls

Black-footed ferret (Photo credit: Kimberly Fraser USFMS)

CHAPTER 21

RECOVERY EFFORTS FOR THE RAREST SHORTGRASS PRAIRIE MAMMAL

K en Morgan is a retired wildlife biologist who worked with the Private Lands Division of Colorado Parks and Wildlife (CPW). Ken has worked on projects to improve habitat for bighorn sheep, elk, sage grouse, and many other species. Ken is a wealth of knowledge and a great storyteller. We interviewed Ken about one of his favorite topics: the efforts to recover the black-footed ferret.

Black-footed ferrets were thought to be extinct but were rediscovered about thirty years ago by a rancher named Mr. Hogg in Meeteetse, Wyoming. Actually, it was Mr. Hogg's dog, Shep, who discovered a black-footed ferret and brought it back to the house. Mr. Hogg said it was a weasel and chucked it into the dead pile. Mr. Hogg's wife was a little bit more curious and took it to a taxidermist. The taxidermist said, "I don't know how to break this to you, but you just brought me an extinct animal."

A group of wildlife biologists went into the Meeteetse Valley and worked to monitor and try to maintain the last remaining ferrets. That is, until sylvatic plague hit, and it came close to wiping out the entire population, the last known black-footed ferrets on Earth.

A group of dedicated scientists made the difficult decision to capture all of the remaining ferrets and put them into captivity. None of us want to make that decision in our careers, but they had to, and they started the captive black-footed ferret breeding program.

The breeding program started in Wyoming. Trying to get black-footed ferrets to breed was a science in itself. The baseline breeding stock came from just seven individuals and, of that, a high percentage of successes were due to one male ferret named Scarface. He was by far the most productive of all.

A ferret recovery center was built south of Carr, Colorado, funded by a bill introduced by Congressman Wayne Allard. There are now nine other sites doing captive breeding, including a number of zoos and the Smithsonian Institution. Some very dedicated scientists brought back that species, which was once considered extinct and is still one of the most endangered mammals in North America.

After the captive breeding program's success, there were socioeconomic issues involved in figuring out how to sustain ferrets in the wild. Black-footed ferrets are predatory animals that feed primarily on prairie dogs. In Colorado, there are three species of prairie dogs: black-tailed prairie dogs, white-tailed prairie dogs, and Gunnison's prairie dogs.

An appropriate site for ferret release needs to have 1,500 acres of black-tailed prairie dogs or 3,000 acres of white-tailed or Gunnison's prairie dogs. Prairie dogs in Colorado are still listed as a noxious rodent pest, and a good portion of the acreage in Colorado occupied by prairie dogs is privately owned. From a rancher's perspective, prairie dogs are

Black-tailed prairie dog

competing with cattle for forage. Ranchers manage grassland on which the cattle depend, and they know the limitation of the carrying capacity of the land.

The Endangered Species Act passed under the Nixon Administration is still considered one of the U.S. Congress's most popular acts ever passed. Yet for many private landowners, especially in the agricultural community, it presents a challenge. If there is an endangered species on your property and you intentionally destroy that species, you can be subject to fines and potentially be shut down. This raises concerns among landowners when the topic of reintroduction of an endangered species is introduced.

The Safe Harbor Agreement, a provision of the Endangered Species Act, has been used to protect both economic interests of landowners and wildlife. It says that if the landowner does everything that they possibly can to maintain an endangered species, they come under no federal restrictions. Under the Safe Harbor agreement provisions, landowners would not be held responsible for ferrets released on their property if they didn't do anything intentionally to harm them.

In addition, a ferret incentive program was initiated: the program compensated landowners, paying up to $20 per acre on a contract that lasted three years, for a minimum of 1,500 acres on acreages where ferrets were reintroduced. The response from ranchers was overwhelmingly positive.

A Colorado law stipulates that it is illegal to reintroduce any endangered species without legislative oversight. Before ferrets could be released in Colorado, CPW had to go before the State Legislature with this proposal. With the provision of holding the landowner free from harm, free from any kind of federal restriction, and the provision of compensation for loss of income, the ferret reintroduction had the overwhelming support of the Colorado Cattlemen's Association and the Colorado Farm Bureau. In a show of support for the program, Terry Fankhauser, the Colorado Cattlemen's Association executive director, sat next to CPW staff at the Colorado State Senate hearing on prairie dog recovery.

One more significant obstacle to releasing ferrets into the wild remained. Sylvatic plague, which is the same pathogen as the bubonic plague that swept through Europe in the fourteenth century, has a devastating impact on both prairie dogs and ferrets.

The plague is not native to the United States. It came in from ships that docked in San Francisco in the 1800s. From there, it moved eastward across the country. A group of research scientists developed a vaccine for prairie dogs. The researchers discovered that prairie dogs love the taste of peanut butter and the colors purple and red. The prairie dogs grabbed the peanut butter bait eagerly, and the colors helped researchers know which animals had been inoculated and which had not. Dusting for fleas (the main vector of the plague) has also proved effective in preventing the spread of plague.

Plague continues to be a limiting factor in the recovery of black-footed ferrets. In addition, the Mustelidae (weasel) family is also highly susceptible to viruses. The COVID-19 virus that has caused a global pandemic in humans has already affected ferrets, weasels, mink, and other members of this family. Ferret recovery centers are quarantining to stop the spread to these animals.

The story of the black-footed ferrets' reintroduction is nothing short of amazing. Beyond that, the unlikely partnership and collaboration with private landowners and the resolution of conflicts between environmental and economic interests within the black-footed ferret program point to something much larger than the recovery of a single species. It represents, perhaps, the best opportunity to conserve and restore shortgrass prairie, one of the most at-risk ecosystems in the United States, as well as the many plant and animal species that are dependent on it.

Local Strategies for the Survival of Species

Ecologists often speak about "keystone species." These are species that play a central role in the lives of other species. Examples of keystone species include alligators in the Everglades that help create shallow sloughs where other species congregate or prairie dogs that provide food for many predators and whose burrows provide habitat for tortoises, burrowing owls, badgers, kit foxes, snakes, and many other species.

Another perspective on species loss is "Jenga theory," which takes its name from a game where participants try to pull pieces from a tower without making it collapse. Jenga theory does not focus on keystone species but says that all species are interdependent, and if enough species are removed from an environmental system, it will eventually collapse. All species are critical, in part because we don't understand all of their complex interrelationships and because too much disruption and too many missing pieces lead to the system's failure.

The suburbitat where we live does not replace the large expanses of intact habitat essential for the survival of wildlife species. The nature where we live is typically made up of novel ecosystems (as previously mentioned in our discussion of suburban open spaces), stormwater ponds, and roof gardens. They are natural areas, however fragmented, that can successfully support some species. Their value is that they allow us to maintain contact with nature. They increase the capacity of

Species Extinction and Human Population

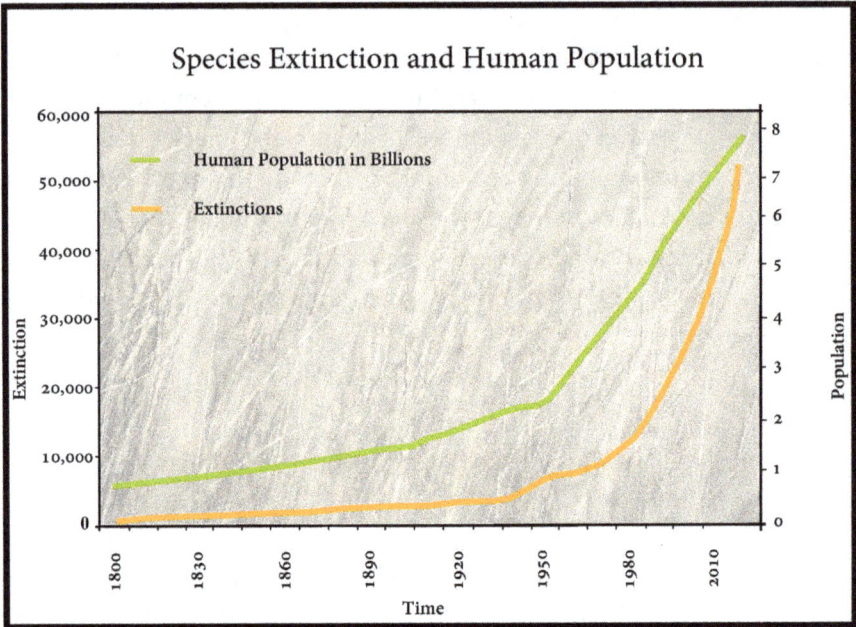

Human population and species extinction (Credit: drawing by J.R. Oldham)

natural systems, and they help build connectivity and create more ways that wildlife can pass through the human domain.

Over the last fifty years, human populations on Earth have doubled. Over the same period, wildlife populations have reduced by roughly half. Here in Colorado, annual Audubon bird counts reveal that bird populations across virtually all species have declined by 60 percent over the last forty years, primarily due to loss of habitat. An Audubon study of the impacts of climate change on North American songbirds presents a dire prediction for a significant loss of habitable range for over 70 percent of bird species on the current trajectory.

When we look around the world, it becomes clear that all extinctions are local. Tigers and elephants are exotic species to us but may be considered a nuisance by local people. It's not that we do not advocate for large-scale global conservation or are willing to write off great apes and other critically endangered species. However, we are specifically charged with the preservation of the wildlife species where we live.

We must dispense with the notion that there is "somewhere else" for wildlife to go. There is nowhere else. Once a site is built on, paved, and landscaped, that habitat is gone forever. With enough time and expense, the habitat could be restored, but even then, it would never be wholly restored to its original condition.

The concept of *Suburbitat*, sharing our world with other species, is critical when human beings occupy so much space. With care and attention, we can preserve, enhance, or create opportunities for wildlife within the environments we design and build.

CHAPTER 22

THE UNIQUELY AMERICAN VOICE OF THE CONSERVATION MOVEMENT

The arrival of European settlers in North America led to a radical alteration of the continent's land use and vegetation. At the same time, the consciousness of European immigrants, and the world, was altered by contact with Native American cultures. Europeans became "Americanized" through exposure to indigenous tribes and, from those tribes, adopted many of the values we consider fundamental to our society. Individuals' rights, democratic leadership, and self-determination were not concepts that fit naturally within European monarchist societies.

Europe of the sixteenth and seventeenth centuries was crowded and environmentally degraded. Its people suffered from a large number of communicable diseases, and the diet of the average person was relatively poor, consisting primarily of grain. Conversely, Native Americans had access to wild game and nutrient-dense wildcrafted foods. The Lakota and Cheyenne people are thought to have been among the largest human beings on Earth during the eighteenth century.

Native American societies did not believe in individual ownership of land, and tribal territories constantly shifted and overlapped. For the first three centuries after they first arrived, Euro-Americans viewed

Henry David Thoreau (Benjamin D. Markham, National Portrait Gallery)

the North American continent's resources as a virtually inexhaustible wealth source to be exploited without reserve. It was not until the mid-nineteenth century that Americans began to see nature as something different: a source of beauty and inspiration.

Henry David Thoreau's *Walden*, published in 1854, was one of the first works of American literature in which the author celebrated the uplifting effects that nature has on the human spirit. Thoreau tells the reader how he built his cabin on the shores of Walden Pond for $28.12. About why he went to the woods, he wrote, "I wished to live deliberately, to front only the essential facts of life, and see if I could not learn

Ralph Waldo Emerson (Library of Congress)

what it had to teach, and not, when I came to die, discover that I had not lived."

Somewhat ironically, while Thoreau chose to live a Spartan existence, close to nature, for a high-minded purpose, he was, in fact, only a short walk away from the town of Concord, Massachusetts. Thoreau was celebrated by an intellectual group of friends, members of the Transcendentalist Movement, who valued simplicity and moral purity. At the same time, from the Appalachian Range westward, settler families eked out a living in the wilderness.

Perhaps it is because he did not live the life-or-death struggle that settler families did that allowed Thoreau to celebrate nature's rejuvenating impact on the human spirit. Far from something to be conquered, Thoreau declared, "In wildness is the preservation of the world."

In the poem "Forbearance," Thoreau's close friend, Ralph Waldo Emerson, defined a conservation ethic in which an individual could appreciate nature without exploiting or destroying it.

Hast thou named all the birds without a gun?
Loved the wood rose, and left it on its stalk?

In the nineteenth century, there was a tradition called the "side hunt" in which every red-blooded American male would go out on Christmas Day and shoot every furred and feathered creature they could find. Sometimes there were contests to see who shot the most birds and animals. Even John James Audubon, for whom the Audubon Society is named, shot virtually every bird he ever painted. The Audubon Christmas Bird Count is a wildlife-friendly adaptation of this tradition.

On March 1, 1871, President Ulysses S. Grant set aside 2,219,791 acres to create Yellowstone, the world's first national park. What exactly a national park was, or should be, and how it was to be managed, was defined after much trial and error over the next century.

John Muir, who was born in Dunbar, Scotland, in 1838, emigrated to the US in 1849. Muir is a well-known champion of wildness because of his writings, particularly about the time that he spent in what would later become Yosemite National Park in California. Muir spoke about the restorative power of nature with a passion that verged on a religious experience. "Everybody needs beauty as well as bread, places to play in and pray in, where nature may heal and give strength to body and soul."

Muir's writings came to the attention of Theodore Roosevelt, and the two became friends. This helped to fuel the acquisition of numerous national parks and a uniquely American concept that the nation's scenic grandeur was every citizen's birthright.

President Ulysses S. Grant (Brady-Handy Photograph Collection, Library of Congress)

John Muir (Library of Congress)

Theodore Roosevelt (Pach Brothers photography studio)

George Bird Grinnell and Aldo Leopold advocated for the conservation of wild species and their habitats, inspired by their experience as hunters and fishermen. Grinnell published *Field and Stream* magazine between 1876 to 1911 and authored numerous books on hunting and American Indian culture.

Aldo Leopold worked for the US Forest Service. Early in Leopold's career, he worked to eradicate wolves and other top predators. Later he came to realize that this did not have the effect of improving herds of game animals. In *A Sand County Almanac,* published in 1949, Leopold writes about the powerfully transformative experience of shooting one of the last wolves in the Gila Wilderness in New Mexico. "We reached the old wolf in time to watch a fierce green fire dying in her eyes. I realized then, and have known ever since, that there was something new to me in those eyes—something known only to her and to the mountain. I was young then, and full of trigger-itch; I thought that because fewer wolves meant more deer, that no wolves would mean hunters' paradise.

George Bird Grinnell (Library of Congress)

But after seeing the green fire die, I sensed that neither the wolf nor the mountain agreed with such a view."

Leopold is best known for his concept of a "land ethic" and is quoted as saying, "When we see land as a community to which we belong, we may begin to use it with love and respect."

The concept of stewarding wildlife and their environments for the benefit of sportsmen, hunters, and fishermen has been tremendously beneficial in environmental stewardship. Ducks Unlimited, a nonprofit focused on protecting and restoring wetland habitat for migratory birds, is primarily funded by hunters.

U.S. Fish and Wildlife Service and state parks and wildlife agencies benefit from entry and license fees paid by sportsmen. It would be a mistake to reduce the motivation of sportsmen as simply a desire to kill wildlife. Few people are as rapturous about the poetry and power of a river as the trout fisherman, who often catch and release fish.

Duck and deer hunters don't get up before dawn, slog through

Aldo Leopold trip to Rio Gavilan (Pacific Southwest Region 5)

wetlands, climb steep mountain paths, or sit in trees and blinds for hours simply for the meat. Many hunters and fishermen have a reverence for the natural world. They seek to be a participant in nature at a level that is uncommon in our society, and they're willing to pay for the privilege.

In many ways, the modern ecology movement can be traced to Rachel Carson, whose *Silent Spring*, published in 1962, alerted the nation to the impacts of pesticides on wildlife and public health. Carson's work was severely criticized within the male-dominated worlds of industry and science. She was mocked and threatened by the agricultural chemical industry for her statements linking pesticides to health impacts such as cancer and wildlife decline. All the while, Carson herself was battling cancer and died in 1964.

Many younger people don't realize how degraded the environment was in the United States in 1970 without environmental protections. In the summer of 1969, the Cuyahoga River in northeast Ohio burned

Rachel Carson (Cornischong at Luxembourgish)

because of the petroleum distillates being dumped into it. Three million gallons of oil spilled in Santa Barbara, California, killing sea life and ruining the beaches. Dioxin and other poisons were dumped into lakes and rivers without regulations. Under President Nixon, the Endangered Species Act and Clean Air Act were passed through bilateral collaboration in Congress within the next two years. The Clean Water Act was later amended and strengthened. As a result of these legislative acts, the aggregate emission of six industrial pollutants decreased by more than 73 percent. For people who can recall the environmental movement of the 1970s, "Save the Whales" has a particular resonance. The phrase was often repeated as a sort of joke. You could identify an "environmental nut" by the Save the Whales sticker on the back of their Volvo.

Whales had been hunted aggressively for centuries. In the eighteenth and nineteenth centuries, whales were hunted primarily for lamp oil. In modern times, whales were (and are) hunted mainly for dog food. Public opinion on whaling changed dramatically when scientists

Humpback whale

recorded whales' sounds and discovered that it was a language; the whales were singing to each other. Few people who have been on a successful whale watch have not been altered by the experience, particularly those who have been fortunate enough to enjoy the thrill of watching whales breaching or bubble-net feeding.

In general, our society tends to focus on crises. If it's not immediate and catastrophic, it doesn't get airtime. For this reason, we tend to miss the celebration of our conservation achievements, and this lack of acknowledgment erodes our confidence. When they hear the word "environment," many people either insist things are awful or roll their eyes, anticipating a moralistic browbeating.

A shortcoming of the environmental movement is that it has often failed in three key areas of engagement:

1. Not engaging the business community in a positive way that honors and encourages the stewardship commitments that companies make.

2. Presenting a vision of the future that is a "gloom and doom" scenario rather than a joyful collaboration with nature.

3. Imagining that there is some kind of moral high ground where individuals can blame companies for the impacts created in the manufacturing and distribution of the products that provide our comfortable lifestyles.

During the 1970s and 1980s, acid rain was one of the most well-known environmental problems in Europe and the United States, particularly in the Northeast. The destruction of coniferous forests and acidification of lakes were very real and presented environmental threats. The problem was primarily due to sulfur dioxide and nitrogen oxides from coal-fired electrical plants. Though acid rain still occurs, the direst projections were never reached because of the actions that have been taken. The impacts were greatly diminished as a result of the United States Air Quality Agreement in 1991 and similar measures in Europe.

The American bald eagle, the symbol of our nation, was reduced to a few hundred pairs in the Lower Forty-eight states in the 1960s. The decline of the bald eagle was directly linked to the use of DDT, a pesticide that concentrated in species at the top of the food chain, which made the shell of the eagle's eggs too thin to survive. Outlawing the use of DDT helped in the recovery of this species, which is now relatively common. At HPEC, we see bald eagles virtually every day in winter when they come to feed on ducks and geese.

Recent decades have seen an increasing awareness of environmental sustainability. Many industries and individual companies have highlighted their "green initiatives" to demonstrate their "social responsibility." This can sometimes (but not always) represent a genuine effort on the part of companies to reduce their carbon footprint, reduce waste, and source materials in a way that causes minimal damage to the environment.

"Sustainable" and "green" can also be just buzzwords that have no real substantiated basis. The term "greenwashing" refers to companies benefiting from an image as an environmental good citizen that is both

Constructed Wetland: a business's goals outpacing a regulatory agency's requirements

unearned and unsubstantiated. Third-party validation of companies can be helpful such as the Blue Fish Label of the Marine Stewardship Council, which verifies for consumers that fish have been sustainably caught.

The U.S. Green Building Council (USGBC) was founded In 1993 by the American Institute of Architects (AIA), with representatives from over sixty firms and nonprofits. In 1998, USGBC launched Leadership in Energy and Environmental Design (LEED), the benchmark for green building. LEED evaluates buildings on energy usage, low toxicity of materials, sustainably harvested materials, and other criteria, and gives the building an overall rating. Builders and business owners can then display the building's rating (bronze, silver, gold, or platinum) as a proclamation of sustainability.

Three distinct strategies are woven through environmental stewardship successes: governmental regulation, informed and engaged consumers, and progressive business models.

At its best, governmental regulation protects the rights of all and minimizes negative impacts on environmental and human health. Informed and engaged consumers have the power to drive companies in the right direction. Progressive businesses can and do often lead the process, raising the bar for sustainability.

An example of a business's goals outpacing a regulatory agency's requirements can be found on the east side of Houts Reservoir at HPEC. A bridge was built in Centerra where Sky Pond Drive passed over an existing wetland. A wetland mitigation project, three times the size of the wetlands that had been impacted, was created as required by the Colorado Department of Health and Environment (CDHE). To verify that the wetland mitigation project was successful, CDHE sent an ecologist out to the site to assess the establishment of the wetlands.

In ecological terms, a wetland must have hydric soils and obligate wetland plant species. The wetland must be wet (flooded or saturated) at least for a portion of the year. Hydric soil is soil that is saturated for long periods and contains anaerobic bacteria. You can often identify hydric soil by cutting into it with a shovel and observing white specks in the soil profile. The other requirement for identifying a wetland is the presence of obligate wetland species, or plants that are only found growing in wetlands.

When the CDHE ecologist came out to inspect the site, the lake levels had been particularly low. The wetland was never inundated, it was dry, with very few plants at all. The inspector did find reed canary grass, an aggressively invasive species that grows in wetlands. This plant was considered an acceptable wetland plant. Had this species alone been planted, it would have hastened the acceptance of the project. The goal of the developer was considerably higher. It was the creation of a diverse wetland plant community.

Having already spent hundreds of thousands of dollars on the wetland project, the developer was faced with the possibility of paying an additional amount in cash to a wetland bank if the project was not accepted. Fortunately the next year was wetter, and the lake levels came up, inundating the wetland and accomplishing the project's goals.

Something extraordinary and unexpected happened later in this wetland. A colony of tulip gentian (*Eustoma grandiflorum*) began to establish all on its own. There may have been a latent seedbed of this plant that was uncovered when the wetland was excavated. The seed, which is as fine as dust, may have been carried in by waterfowl. Whatever the case, in years when conditions are right, a purple sea of these flowers explodes into bloom in late July.

Wetland bench construction

The next year was wetter, and the lake levels came up

The US joined 195 other parties to sign the Paris Agreement, an international treaty to address climate change, in 2015. The United States government filed its intent to withdraw from the Paris Agreement, on November 4, 2019, (the US rejoined the agreement in 2021). However, many states and businesses continued to focus on the carbon reduction goals they have set for themselves.

Xcel Energy has committed to reducing carbon output levels by 80 percent by 2030 and becoming 100 percent carbon-free by 2050. The plan includes retiring twenty-three coal-burning plants between 2005 and 2027, roughly half of the utility's coal-fired plants. Coal-fired plants will be replaced with cleaner, renewable energy sources, such as wind and solar power. The company is implementing the country's largest multistate wind power plan, which trades energy production with other states, depending on where the wind may be blowing.

A more controversial aspect of the plan includes the ongoing operation of two nuclear plants, which provide 30 percent of the energy consumed by their customers in the Upper Midwest. The company also does not take the construction of "a new breed of smaller nuclear plants" off the table.

Of course, all forms of energy production, including solar and wind, have potentially negative impacts on wildlife. The company (as must all public utilities) must regularly monitor bird collisions at their wind farms and follow strict wildlife protection guidelines under federal laws. These include the Endangered Species Act, The Migratory Bird Treaty Act, and the Bald and Golden Eagle Protection Act. High-tension wires themselves were a source of eagle deaths in the past until utilities began spacing wires further apart, preventing electrocution.

American presidents have created many national monuments through executive orders. Creating national monuments and national parks has often met with resistance from local people who did not see until later the economic benefit that these tourist areas provide to their communities. The federal government's role is to look at the big picture and long-term benefit to the people, beyond private interests and short term uses.

In 1883, British economist William Forster Lloyd wrote about the "tragedy of the commons." The essay was meant to support private ownership and used the example of common areas becoming degraded

Tulip gentian (*Eustoma grandiflorum*)

by unregulated grazing. In this context, the tragedy of the commons means that when land is not held privately and is not any particular party's legacy or responsibility, it tends to become degraded, overused, and abused.

The phrase "tragedy of the commons" is often discussed in academic circles to highlight a slightly different point: people's tendency to abdicate responsibility for stewardship of land and resources that are not their own. In other words, without regulation, business interests may exhaust resources or degrade the environment on publicly owned lands.

Elinor Ostrom, an American, was awarded the Nobel Prize in Economics for demonstrating in her book, *Governing the Commons*, the ways that some communities have managed to avoid the collapse of natural resources, such as fisheries, through cooperation and self-regulation.

At the High Plains Environmental Center, we share the frustrations that all managers of open space experience. We have found animals such as snakes and toads killed by trail users. We have discovered

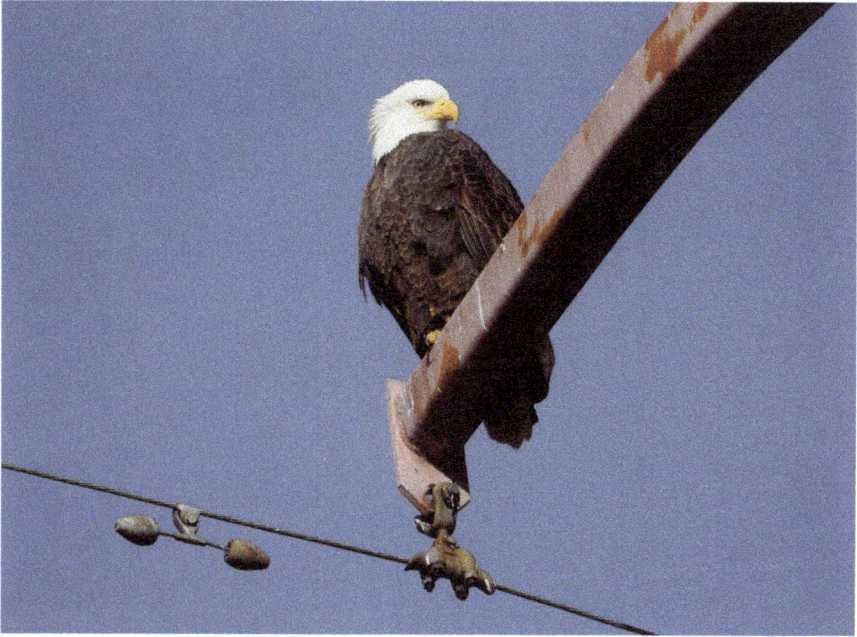

Bald eagles often perch on powerlines.

robins that went for the wrong worm, hanging in trees suspended by fishing lines and hooks. We experience vandalism, theft, and the typical wear and tear that all open spaces endure.

When these things happen, we do our best to clean up and put back together. As Stephen Mather, the first director of the National Park System, said when confronted with complaints about so many people using the park and leaving their trash behind, "So, we can pick up the trash, it's a cheap way of making good citizens."

An even better way to make good citizens is to engage the community in cleaning up the natural area, an effort that we lead multiple times each year.

CHAPTER 23

ECOLOGY AND ECONOMY

The hardest work of social engagement is working with our own opinions, our biases, and our assumptions about other people. A fundamental obstacle for the environmental movement since its early days in the late 1960s and early 1970s is an imaginary moral high ground that transfers responsibility for the environment to the business community.

There's a disconnect when we see a "no fracking" sign in front of a huge house with that thirsty, chemical-laden lawn, and two SUVs in the driveway. We need to reframe this discussion in a way that we can assume our collective responsibility, free from blame, and engage in an authentic dialog about how to achieve the lifestyle we want without destroying the planet we live on.

That is not to say that businesses are not capable of cynical, even criminal, actions. A botanist we know was hired to identify rare native plants on a site slated for development. The botanist marked the plants with great care, and every single plant was immediately, and mysteriously, destroyed so that they would not become an obstacle to development. This is where an informed and engaged public opinion is helpful. The vast majority of people, developers included, abhor such behavior.

The business community is often the leader for environmental stewardship. People sometimes speak about developers as being profit-driven and callous about the impacts of their projects. Our experience is often quite the contrary.

Colorado is one of the leading states in the U.S. for LEED construction. This is most likely because of universities in the area, as well as a business community that is inspired to do what is the most progressive, innovative, and state of the art, and to make that part of their story. Developers are often quick to see the advantage of building smaller units with shared walls and more open space surrounding them or utilizing water-saving native lawns. They take on a risk, when implementing these approaches, that the public will be informed enough and willing to come along with these environmentally friendly innovations.

Discussions of whether people with the means should be allowed to own houses spanning tens of thousands of square feet, private jets, or other examples of conspicuous wealth and consumption, would be better focused on individuals or organizations paying the actual cost of these things. The actual cost would include the repair of environmental damage caused by extraction, manufacturing, distribution, and disposal of products.

Often resources are extracted from areas with poor or underrepresented people. The environments that these people live in are often degraded or destroyed, and the condition of the people, wildlife, and vegetation is diminished in the process.

Ecology and economy are related words from the Greek root "*oikos*," meaning household. Ecology is the study of the house, and economy is the management of the house. Ecological and economic best practices are usually in alignment if the true costs of goods, including the environmental cost, and resource depletion are calculated. In this reckoning of costs, the "commons" are the natural resources and the environment itself, which belongs to all life forms, present and future.

Understanding the economic benefits of environmental stewardship, including cost comparisons with conventional landscaping, and implementing a more regionally appropriate style, is a perfectly legitimate and no-less-noble reason to adapt our landscapes to be more environmentally sound. In fact, economics is perhaps the best reason because cost comparison is likely to produce pragmatic results among developers and municipalities on a large scale (and by the way, conserving natural resources literally saves the world).

How then do we create a broad-based alignment around the issues of environmental stewardship? Although we have had notable successes in restoring parts of our environment, the younger generation faces some of the greatest environmental challenges, with climate change, melting ice caps, and mass extinction, as well as threats to our growing human population such as drought, hunger, homelessness, and war. The fact is, we already have everything we need to tackle these challenges—the scientific knowledge, technology, money, and nature's tremendous power for regeneration, healing, and growth. What we lack as a society is the collective will to undertake this work, the understanding of why this is so critically important, the ability to communicate our vision, and the tolerance to work with individuals with widely divergent points of view and interests.

To begin, it is necessary for us to overcome polarization and recover a sense of common purpose in our fragmented society. The only way to create a better society is for us to become better citizens collectively and individually. As idealistic as this may sound, we are a relatively young species that has gained an enormous amount of control over our environment. We have managed to forestall the feedback loops that species experience when they deplete or degrade their environment, but that feedback is rapidly gaining on us.

At this point we either grow up or die out, possibly destroying many other species in the process. We cannot afford to live without the ecosystem services that nature provides us, and we are faced with the question of whether we have the right to destroy the ability of our own species to survive.

This then becomes a discussion of morality and ethics, which is beyond the scope of science alone. As Gus Spaeth, scientist, environmental lawyer, and US advisor on climate change, said, "I used to think that top environmental problems were biodiversity loss, ecosystem collapse, and climate change. I thought that thirty years of good science could address these problems. I was wrong. The top environmental problems are selfishness, greed, and apathy, and to deal with these we need a cultural and spiritual transformation. And we scientists don't know how to do that."

CHAPTER 24

A CONSERVATION ETHIC FOR THE TWENTY-FIRST CENTURY

I f you found an injured bird on the ground, you would probably be concerned about it. You might pick it up, put it in a shoebox with some grass, and try to feed it. Perhaps you might call someone to get advice, or bring it to a wildlife rehabilitation center. We relate to our world personally.

We would like to think that we wish animals well and that we would help them if they were in trouble. Most adults would not harm an animal needlessly. But it takes a leap of understanding to advocate for wild animal populations and for the preservation of the natural areas on which they depend.

The life of a wild animal is difficult. It involves a constant search for food, often unsuccessfully. For many species, there is the constant threat of predators. In addition, the numbers of animals killed on roads, birds killed in window strikes or by household pets, and collateral damage to pollinators from pesticide use is in the tens of millions, if not billions, of animals in the United States every year.

The Audubon Society took 140 million observations from birders and scientists to map where 604 American bird species live. Using current climate models to show how those ranges will shift due to climate change, Audubon concluded that 389 North American bird species face extinction from loss of their existing habitable range.

Older Americans may remember having to stop on a road trip to scrape bugs off the windshield. Cars on similar trips now may arrive without a speck, but what does that say for our bird population that depends on insects for food?

Yet species can recover as a result of human awareness or intervention. Many pollinating insects, which have brief life spans, can replenish their numbers in just one or two seasons when beneficial practices are implemented. This primarily involves planting the right forage plants and reducing or eliminating harmful chemicals.

Human activities have often had disastrous results on wildlife and their environments through direct action such as overhunting or as a secondary result of habitat destruction. Yet many human beings have dedicated their lives to conservation, sometimes even putting their lives at risk, as in the case of divers who have worked to cut whales free from entanglement in crab traps.

If we have the scientific knowledge to resolve many of the world's ecological problems. Why then have we not been more successful in implementing them? Over the last sixty years, the population of wildlife across the Earth has declined by more than half and, at the same time, the population of human beings has doubled. For that reason, some scientists refer to this period of time when humans are the dominant element in global ecology as the "Anthropocene." The Earth will survive with or without human beings. Our success in dominating other species, which has led us to be on the path to mass extinction, may ultimately result in our own extinction due to the loss of critical ecosystem services that plants and wildlife provide. Diversity in nature, like the diversity of human cultures, creates more opportunity. A decline in species diversity increases the threat of environmental collapse. Beyond that, the loneliness of living in a dead world could be the undoing of our emotional and psychological health.

How then could we evolve and harness the best of human potential in the race against time to save nature? How can we as individuals become effective advocates for, and practitioners of, environmental stewardship?

The process for us to become good citizens and stewards of this planet includes three essential components. First we must care about

Bee balm (*Monarda fistulosa*) and fritillary butterfly

our own survival and recognize our obligation to the welfare of others. We need to have the correct information for our actions to be effective. Most importantly, we need to take action and sustain our ongoing commitment to this work.

Motivation

In order to benefit nature, it is first necessary that we care. Empathy, caring for others, is an essential building block of human relationships. It's a bond that creates families, communities, and societies. We are taught from the earliest age to play nicely with others. At a certain point, we may develop mirror neurons, which may cause us to wince when we see someone hurt themselves, bring tears to our eyes when we see someone cry, or laugh when others are laughing.

Empathy is a foundational value of the world's spiritual traditions. Not causing harm, helping others in need, and forgiveness are often taught (though not always followed) as religious tenets. However there is often no specific direction given to guide our interactions with the natural world.

The world's great religious teachings arose in a time before the present global environmental crisis existed. Many religious groups are currently examining their own traditions to see what they may contain that may be of benefit to the current global situation. The identification of specific problems such as air and water pollution are common themes in the discussion about environmental stewardship. These are symptomatic problems that point to the greater disconnect that takes place in the hearts and minds of human beings.

Thich Nhat Han, a Vietnamese Buddhist monk writes, "Our way of walking on the earth has a great influence on animals and plants. We have killed so many animals and plants and destroyed their environments. Many are now extinct. In turn our environment is now harming us. We are like sleepwalkers, not knowing what we are doing or where we are heading. Whether we can wake up or not depends on whether we can walk mindfully on our mother earth. The future of all life, including our own, depends on our mindful steps."

The Asian traditions of Hinduism and Buddhism talk about *karma*, the direct result of actions. *Ahimsa*, refraining from causing harm, is a primary focus of the Jain religion. These spiritual principles have led to a tolerance for, and even active protection of monkeys, cranes, and other Asian wildlife species even in the midst of cities. However, in the book, *Ethics for 21st Century*, H.H. Dalai Lama says of his native Tibet, "Nowhere are the consequences of our failure to exercise discipline in the way we relate to our environment more apparent than in the case of present-day Tibet. It is no exaggeration to say that the Tibet I grew up in was a wildlife paradise. Every traveler who visited Tibet before the middle of the twentieth century remarked on this. Animals were rarely hunted except in the areas where crops could not be grown. Indeed, it was customary for government officials annually to issue a proclamation protecting wildlife . . . sadly this profusion of wildlife is no longer to be found. Partly due to hunting but primarily due to loss of habitat, what remains half a century after Tibet was occupied is only a fraction of what there was . . . None of this is to say that historically we Tibetans were deliberately "conservationist." We were not. The idea of something called "pollution" never occurred to us. A small population inhabited a very large area with clean, dry air and an abundance of pure mountain water. This innocent attitude toward cleanliness meant that when we Tibetans went into exile, we were astonished to discover for example, the existence of streams whose water was not drinkable."

Much of the predominant view of the environment in Western societies is based on the verse found in Genesis 1:26 (King James Version) that states man is given "dominion over the fish of the sea, over the fowl of the air, and over the cattle, and over all the earth, and over every creeping thing that creepeth upon the earth."

In the book *The Ten Trusts*, Jane Goodall and Marc Becoff argue, "Some Hebrew scholars believe that "dominion" is a poor translation of the word *v'yrida* which means to 'rule over' in the sense of a wise king ruling over his subjects with enlightened stewardship."

Could we perhaps have gotten it wrong on a very fundamental level that the earth is not here just for us to use, but to care for as well? Understanding the difference between those two things is an essential component of any healthy relationship. If we have not reached the stage where other people, let alone wild beings, matter to us personally, we have considerable unrealized potential for personal and spiritual growth.

Pope Francis frequently talks about the duty of humanity to protect the environment, as well as vulnerable human populations impacted by climate change, "We are faced not with two separate crises, one environmental and the other social, but rather with one complex crisis which is both social and environmental. Strategies for a solution demand an integrated approach to combating poverty, restoring dignity to the excluded, and at the same time protecting nature."

Rick Warren, evangelical leader, and author of *The Purpose Driven Life,* put it this way, "Life is all about stewardship. It all belongs to God—he just loans it to us for a short period of time. The first command God gave to man was to take care of the Earth, which includes managing and protecting the environment."

Knowledge

Our motivation may be ignited by common sense, economics, or a spiritual epiphany about the interdependence of all living things. To be truly effective in our goal to preserve the natural world, it is necessary to join motivation together with an intellectual understanding of the way that nature actually works, illuminated by scientific evidence. We may otherwise be motivated on an emotional level without having good information, and our activities may not only be ineffective, they could actually be counterproductive to our goals.

For example, a practice in the Buddhist tradition of releasing animals is motivated by the belief that all sentient beings have been our mother in a previous existence. The practice is said to generate "merit" for the one who releases the animal.

A Japanese story tells about a monk who sees a turtle weeping in the marketplace. Moved by pity, the monk buys the turtle and sets it free. Later, the monk falls overboard at sea, and the very same turtle lifts him up, saves him from drowning, and carries him safely to the shore.

However we live in a world that has become much more complicated than that. We have heard of people doing this animal release practice by purchasing fish in a pet store and releasing them into lakes and streams. From an ecological perspective, no one should ever release any kind of pet into the wild. A pet is not likely to survive when released into the wild, or worse, they might survive and become an invasive species.

Modern scientific methods have their roots in the Renaissance period when people set aside beliefs and pursued questions with an open-minded curiosity. Science is based on testing a theory through experimentation and the collection of data. Scientists speak in terms of probabilities, not beliefs. For that reason, theories change as information changes. Belief, on the other hand, is an adherence to a particular view independent of demonstrable facts.

Scientific theories are the result of evidence-based research which is then tested and reviewed by peers in the scientific community before being accepted. People may point to the fact that scientific understanding changes when new evidence is presented. Adapting to new information is the foundation of the scientific approach. Holding on to beliefs that have been disproven is dogma, not science.

Science is not perfect or invulnerable to corruption. There have been instances where business interests have suppressed or distorted scientific research, as in the case of cigarette smoking and its connection with lung cancer.

The solution to this problem is more science, not less. We need more publicly funded research, we need to allow that research to drive environmental policies and legislation, and we need to reinvest in educating our population.

We live in a dangerous period where half-baked theories and conspiracies abound. For us to be successful in stewarding the environment, we need to find points of agreement based on verifiable facts. Peer-reviewed science is our best tool for achieving this.

Some people have held up the knowledge of indigenous people as an example of alternate ways of "knowing" that somehow vie with science. The knowledge that indigenous people have gained about managing the environment is based on centuries of solid observation and experience. It is science.

This is not to say that intuition has no role in science or in developing solutions to challenging problems. Intuition and dreams can provide profound and spontaneous insights and have often contributed to scientific theories. In a democratic society, policies need to be rooted in verifiable facts and broad agreement on implementing solutions.

It is not uncommon for people of differing political persuasions to refute science when it does not support their opinions. For example, some people may claim GMOs (genetically modified organisms) and herbicides are harmful to human and ecological health without substantiating these claims with scientific evidence. Other people may challenge statements about the ways that human activities have contributed to climate change as being false, although 99 percent of the world's scientific community accept this as the probable cause.

Vaccinations, which have helped to control many of the world's most deadly diseases, seem to meet resistance from a segment of the population regardless of political persuasion. Conspiracy theories abound, including a claim that birds are really government drones, that trails left by airplanes in flight are actually chemicals intended to control people's behavior, and that human beings never actually landed on the moon.

Belief in unsubstantiated claims, and the refusal to accept legitimate science, are obstacles to achieving the goals of environmental stewardship.

Action

Action is the final, and perhaps most important element for successful stewardship of the natural world. As Thomas Edison said, "Genius is 1 percent inspiration and 99 percent perspiration."

We once worked with a group of college students who were eager to save the Earth. They wanted to help with environmental stewardship projects and to learn. After days of weeding invasive plants and pushing a wheelbarrow, they became bored and frustrated as if they thought the work was going to be more glamorous than this, but it isn't. Stewardship is hard work. It requires tremendous patience and application, as well as a willingness to keep going in the face of failures and loss. Action includes challenging our own assumptions, checking our biases, and engaging in dialog with people and perspectives that are sometimes outside of our comfort zone to build broad-based collaboration. Solutions often come from unexpected places. It's necessary that we keep an open mind so that we can recognize them when we see them.

In addition, action means social action. For too long, people with intelligence, motivation, and innovation have not been able to advance their ideas due to a lack of opportunity and our society has suffered for it. We need *everyone*, from every ethnic and socioeconomic background, to find solutions to the world's most pressing problems.

The process of governance and legislation is another example of the need for exertion. Creating laws and regulations is a tedious, difficult, and frankly, boring process, and generally no one gets everything they want. People seem to vote for the politician of their choice and almost inevitably they become frustrated because their candidate doesn't accomplish everything they promise, or they begin to compromise.

The goals of environmental stewardship may advance at an uneven pace, but we must progress. At HPEC, we operate based on periodic strategic planning sessions. Sometimes after months and years of hard work, we look up and we're surprised to see what we've accomplished. Rereading our strategic plan reminds us that we have traveled a very intentional path toward our goals.

CHAPTER 25

THE COURAGE TO ACT

Houses and wildfire smoke

"What is the use of a house if you haven't got
a tolerable planet to put it on?"

—Henry David Thoreau

We began writing this book in the summer of 2020, when hundreds of thousands of acres of forests were burning throughout the West. In cities along the Front Range, fumes and smoke hung in the air so thickly at times that it created an otherworldly light. Air quality was in the poor to dangerous range off and on from August through much of October.

The communities that we design and build need to have a positive effect on natural areas and resources, or nature will have a negative effect on us. If we contribute to climate change or environmental degradation, it will eventually impact our lifestyle. In ecological terms, this is called a feedback loop.

Water supplies in much of the West are dependent on high altitude forests that trap and release snowfall. The decline of forests through an increased fire cycle, and the forest's inability to regenerate due to climate change, are critical concerns. In addition, municipal water departments have observed, after previous fires, that erosion has diminished water quality and ash raises the acidity level of water, which causes corrosion of pipes and other concerns.

Our landscapes can help wildlife to survive during periods of drought. This summer, the gardens around HPEC were thronging with birds and pollinators. Hummingbirds, which are usually found at higher elevations in summer, buzzed through our gardens in record numbers. Songbirds flocked to our gardens as well, seeking fruit, flowers, and insects when many other sites were barren and dry. Hiking in the mountains to find wildflower seeds yielded nothing because many plants had flowered little, or not at all.

After the long summer's drought, a sudden deep cold in early September sent millions of birds in the Rocky Mountain West into a migration for which they were not prepared. Tens of thousands, perhaps hundreds of thousands, of birds were found dead in Southwestern states, where birds literally dropped from the sky.

A subsequent necropsy confirmed that the birds had died of starvation, unable to gain sufficient weight before migrating. As the effects of climate change increase occurrences such as this, it increases the need for us to subsidize the diet of our wild birds. Creating habitat within the landscapes that we design could make an enormous difference to their survival.

The period in which we find ourselves has been described as a "bottleneck" in which the needs of a growing human population and a rising standard of living combine to deplete resources, damage the environment, and accelerate the extinction of species. In the best-case scenario, the bottleneck would give way to a period of stabilized pop-

Hummingbirds are frequently drawn to tubular-shaped garden flowers.

Holding one tiny bird while thousands of others flocked to our gardens under a smoke-filled sky.

ulation growth, sustainable technologies, and long-term conservation of habitat and resources. In the words of E.O. Wilson, author of *The Future of Life*, "If there is a universal environmental ethic, it is that life on Earth should be preserved." To that we would add the diversity of species and their habitats should be preserved.

As we've discussed, since human populations and their impacts cover virtually every part of the globe, all extinctions are local to someone. Many people living in Colorado have moved from places where there is more water. Beyond that, many of us are descendants of settlers who came from cool and rain-soaked environments in Northern Europe. Although emerald green may feel right to us on some deep ancestral level, the time has come for us to learn to love this land for its own unique beauty, and in so doing, become a deeper part of it. Our ability to survive in this land called *Ȟe Ská*, (the shining mountains) by the Lakota, is largely dependent on our ability to love it for what it is.

In no sense are we arguing for austerity. This is rather an invitation to celebrate landscapes that are vibrant and interesting year-round, in a way that allows other beings, present and future, to do the same. We have observed firsthand how dramatically and rapidly our local birds and pollinators recover when we grow native plants in our gardens. This book is a declaration that Colorado and the Rocky Mountain West is (or was) beautiful and good in its natural state. Celebrating our native biodiversity can restore our relationship to the land and may allow the new civilization that we have built on this land to continue, in harmony with nature.

This leads us to the fundamental question of what constitutes a good human life. Human beings, like other species, require food, water, shelter, and space. In addition, like many other animals, human beings require interaction with others of our species. Human beings are social in nature. Families are the building blocks of communities, and communities are the building blocks of nations. Many human beings, unlike any other species that we know of, require a life with meaning and connection. This is expressed to varying degrees and in different ways by people around the world.

In the 1980s, Joseph Campbell, who had studied and written about mythology from cultures around the world, was interviewed by Bill

Late summer garden at HPEC featuring horsetail milkweed (*Asclepias subverticillata*), Bigelow's tansy aster (*Machaeranthera bigelovii*), smooth sumac (*Rhus glabra*).

Moyers. At one point in the interview, Campbell told a story about a policeman in Hawaii who had risked his own life to save a young man who was attempting to commit suicide by jumping off a cliff. The police officer, who almost lost his own life, was interviewed by a local newspaper. When asked why he had risked his life, the officer said, "If I had let go of that young man's hand, I could not have lived with myself for one more day."

When we live life with such a sense of purpose, we can become truly fearless. A parent seeing their child in danger of being struck by a moving car doesn't stop to think *Should I risk danger to myself?* They simply act. Love and a sense of belonging give us the courage to act. A human life is short. What gives life meaning if not an allegiance to the protection of life itself? The more we love, the more we realize how little we are risking and how much we have to gain. In the absence of self-fixation, we become truly great.

Twenty-first century conservation includes leveraging opportunities to bring wildness back into the communities that we design and build. This puts nature back in the lives of people, providing an opportunity for improving our mental and physical health and connecting people with a sense of place—nature literally on our doorstep.

In order to be successful, we need to create better alignment and reignite our sense of citizenship and stewardship in our local communities, our nation, and the global community. Our efforts to promote the use of native plants in gardening and the restoration of natural areas is much more than a local concern. It is a fundamental building block for stewarding nature, creating connection between our wildlife and human neighbors, and bequeathing a cleaner, healthier, and more beautiful world to future generations.

ABOUT THE AUTHOR

Jim Tolstrup

Jim Tolstrup is executive director of the High Plains Environmental Center in Loveland, Colorado, a unique model for preserving native biodiversity in the midst of development. His past work experience includes serving as Land Stewardship director of Shambhala Mountain Center in Red Feather Lakes, Colorado, and running his own landscape design business in Kennebunkport, Maine, where he installed gardens at George and Barbara Bush's "Summer White House."

Jim holds a Certificate in Gardening Arts from Harvard University and the Arnold Arboretum. He has written numerous articles on gardening and environmental stewardship for various publications, and is a past recipient of Denver Water's Xeriscape Award, ALCC's Excellence in Landscaping Merit Award, ASLA Land Stewardship Award, and the Sustainable Living Association's Sustainable Contribution Award.

Growing up in an urban environment near Boston, Massachusetts, Jim had to "look hard to find nature." This background led to a strong sense of empathy for people, and children in particular, who don't have access to the restorative qualities of nature in their daily lives.

Jim is personally committed to bringing together people with diverse points of view (environmentalists, business people, and other community members) in an inclusive dialogue about preserving the natural world for future generations.

As a founder and former president of Cankatola Tiospaye, a nonprofit that provides material assistance to Native American elders, Jim has gained a perspective through lifelong friendships with Native Americans living on reservations in South Dakota and elsewhere, that the land we live on is much more than a commodity, it is a community of which mankind is an integral part.

www.ingramcontent.com/pod-product-compliance
Lightning Source LLC
Chambersburg PA
CBHW051712020426
42333CB00014B/952